THE ECONOMICS OF THE PARABLES

The Economics *of the* Parables

Robert Sirico

**Author of *Defending the Free Market* and
*A Moral Basis for Liberty***

REGNERY GATEWAY
Washington, D.C.

Regnery Gateway™ is a trademark of Salem Communications Holding
Corporation
Regnery® is a registered trademark and its colophon is a trademark of
Salem Communications Holding Corporation

Cataloging-in-Publication data on file with the Library of Congress

ISBN: 978-1-68451-242-3
eISBN: 978-1-68451-291-1
Library of Congress Control Number: 2021949816

Published in the United States by
Regnery Gateway, an imprint of
Regnery Publishing
A division of Salem Media Group
Washington, D.C.
www.Regnery.com

Manufactured in the United States of America

10 9 8 7 6 5 4 3 2 1

Books are available in quantity for promotional or premium use.
For information on discounts and terms, please visit our website:
www.Regnery.com.

For Robert J. Powers

A friend, gentleman, and entrepreneur who embodied the values expressed in this work. R.I.P.

Contents

A Note on the Use of the
King James Version of the Bible

G iven what some might perceive to be the oddity of a Catholic priest electing to use the Authorized or King James Version of the Bible in the course of this study of the parables, I thought it prudent to offer the reasons for my choice.

The reader will immediately see from the various sources I have employed throughout the text that I have endeavored to make this book widely accessible to a diverse and interfaith audience. I simply want to reach as many people, from all religious approaches, as possible. Yet, that is not the reason I chose to use the KJV.

Despite being raised in an Italian-American Catholic household, my upbringing in Brooklyn, New York, afforded me diverse experiences and friendships. In my teens I went to lots of Protestant churches with my friends. It was there, especially at Black Pentecostal churches, that I first learned to love Black gospel music and the cadence of the KJV Bible.

I grant that the KJV is not the easiest translation for many people to follow, in the same way that some people find Shakespeare difficult. It is not even, given modern scholarship, the most accurate and useful translation for serious study. But its capacity to evoke devotion and reverence and the use of what some have called "Biblical English" in the KJV, helps to capture the style of the original Hebrew and Greek, and is especially suited for the forceful and majestic dialogue of the parables and the lessons they contain.

The Enduring Power of the Parables

L ibraries are filled with books on the parables of Christ, and rightly so. Here we have stories full of surprising details and challenging conclusions that offer moral direction of great potency. They cause us to pause and think. "There is no doubt that the parables constitute the heart of Jesus' preaching," wrote Pope Emeritus Benedict XVI. "While civilizations have come and gone, these stories continue to teach us anew with their freshness and their humanity."[1]

Many of their lessons are counterintuitive. They are more difficult to understand than we might initially expect. And yet we tend to remember them. Many of them long ago entered into the popular imagination and have stayed there, even in highly secularized times, detached from their contexts. While they are stories kindred with fables, legends, folklores, allegories, and myths; parables—and the parables of Jesus in particular—are something more because they so readily prompt us to examine our hearts and think through eternal matters from the perspective of the whole of Christ's teaching and person, by way of practical examples from our daily experience.

The Latin word *parabola* is derived from the Greek *parabolē*, meaning to throw, or put by the side of, or place side by side. The word was used by Plato and Socrates to mean a comparative story, a

Christ Preaching by Rembrandt. *Library of Congress*

fictitious analogy designed to reveal a deeper truth.[2] Seneca says that
parables are necessary to the proper demonstration of truth.[3] The
Talmud includes parables too, elaborating on their use in the Hebrew
scriptures.[4]

Parables have been used throughout history as rhetorical or teaching devices. But the parables of Jesus are not merely didactic; they
convey transcendent meaning not to be found on their surface, and
the implications of the parables change according to the audience.
This is precisely the point of a parable: a story leading to a deeper
meaning. "He that hath ears to hear, let him hear," Jesus would say
(Mark 4:9).[5] His parables demand our engagement and our choice.

There was a political backdrop to the parabolic approach to
teaching. Jesus' public ministry took place amidst an atmosphere of
political and religious danger. The Roman state, like all states, wanted

no competitors and was quick to judge anyone it so regarded as an enemy. Jesus' fellow Jews awaited the Messiah, but their leaders had every interest in prolonging the wait as long as possible.

So how could Jesus convey his teachings in a way that would be understood with precision by those open to his message, and at the same time not alarm those without ears to hear, thus inciting controversy that would distract from his principal focus? His parables were part of the answer. "Therefore speak I to them in parables," he said, "because they seeing see not; and hearing they hear not, neither do they understand" (Matthew 13:13).

Jesus "wants to show how something they have hitherto not perceived can be glimpsed via a reality that does fall within their range of experience," explains Benedict XVI. "By means of [a] parable he brings something distant within their reach so that, using the parable as a bridge, they can arrive at what was previously unknown."[6]

The parable must be distinguished from pure allegory. Parables deal with a piece of real life, something that might very well have happened, whereas allegory is more likely to deal with pure fantasy in order to illustrate a metaphorical meaning. Parables teach on two levels: the real-life message and the theological analog. In order to comprehend the fullness of the message, both must be understood.

Leopold Fonck, whose classic work on Jesus' parables is noteworthy, argues that a parable in the Christian sense has four elements: 1) the discourse has an internal independence and completeness, so that it makes sense on its own, 2) it must point to a supernatural truth, 3) this truth must be clothed in figurative language, and 4) the two must be compared.[7]

One can hear the parables as a follower who believes Jesus to be the Son of God. Or one can hear them as a person who regards the teacher to be a great moral figure. One may even hear the parables for their literary or rhetorical force alone. And one can hear the story in its most plain and mundane meaning and still gain insight. Some do not require any explanation. Yet deep reflection is required of them all.

Parables are most often discussed in terms of their higher meaning, and surely that is the primary idea and goal. To hear and repeat a wonderful story while missing its larger purpose and lesson defeats the point of the parable. Yet it remains true that the parables of Jesus are classic stories in and of themselves. The moral and spiritual significance of their lessons can be deepened and more clearly elucidated if we develop a richer understanding of the circumstances, logic, presuppositions, and meaning of the stories themselves.

The enduring power of the stories themselves is striking. The world of two thousand years ago is almost unimaginably different from our own in so many ways. None of the technologies that drive our daily life were in existence. Living standards were immeasurably lower. Lifespans were vastly shorter. Ideas about prosperity, class mobility, security, and life vulnerability in general were inconceivably different then. The people of biblical times did not carry around with them the ideas that we take for granted in our times, such as universal human rights, political equity, or fundamental freedoms. Nor, for that matter, did they have access to people around the globe via a small device in the folds of their tunics.

And yet the examples in the stories retain the ring of authenticity. After all, people still fish, dive for pearls, tend grape vines, sow seed and reap crops, store up harvests, adjudicate inheritances and gifts, build houses with foundations, pay debts (or don't), struggle with income disparity, encounter the poor in their midst, endure inter-family tensions, and experience many of the other variations of life one finds in the parables. The power of the parables endures in part because the examples Jesus chose have proven to be persistent throughout history. They are part of the enduring human condition, while retaining a freshness that prevents them from seeming old fashioned or "old tech" at all. They appeal to something natural, constant, and ubiquitous in human experience.

As someone who regularly writes and speaks publicly, I am attentive to provide enduring examples of the abstract lessons I may want to convey, and I find myself in awe of this feature of Jesus' parables. (I say this not merely as a priest, but as someone who frequently finds himself before secular audiences.) Ask any communicator to come up with stories that will still make sense a decade after they are told, and he will admit the challenge. One highly regrettable feature of contemporary homiletics is the recognition of the power of parabolic preaching in combination with the failure, perhaps from a lack of patience, to come up with a story that actually communicates the message one wants to deliver. We have all heard a preacher begin a homily or sermon with a compelling story or an attention-grabbing joke, only to be let down when, having listened to the end, we discover the introduction had nothing to do with the core of his message.

And for a story to demonstrate resiliency over two thousand years is at an entirely higher order altogether. In the current cultural landscape, it is hard to see if people are any longer capable of distinguishing the permanent things from transient occurrences. A parable from fifteen years ago, for example, might involve a reference to a video tape or a floppy disc. How many today would miss the meaning of the reference, or the intrinsic connection between the image and the message, let alone any subtler nuance? Jesus' parables are rarely so obscured, even if it is occasionally helpful to clarify some unique cultural or linguistic detail.

One of the reasons the parables remain so compelling is that there are certain fundamental truths about the economic dimension of life that remain unchanged, even given the changes in technology, demographics, and lifestyles from two thousand years ago to the present. It is, after all, still the case that nature does not provide enough in the way of resources to meet all human needs at any one moment. Resources have grown enormously, and yet they remain scarce in comparison to human needs and desires. That means that we will always have to face the reality of scarcity—and the problem of the production, creation and allocation of goods and services to serve human needs. Wealth is not given; it must be created. And there are more successful and less successful ways of achieving that.

Then once wealth is created, we must face the inevitable moral dilemmas about how it is to be allocated. The fundamental fact of scarcity in this world confronts us with both practical and moral issues concerning ownership, responsibility, waste, and efficiency. We must also constantly confront the forward passage of time as an economic constraint, a reality all too often simply ignored. (This may well be the origin of the phrase "time is money.") There are trade-offs: the accumulation versus the distribution of wealth, the here and now versus the longer term, and, of course, between the temporal and the eternal. In this vale of tears there will always be a struggle between provision for material life and the interior preparation for the next.

These choices, trade-offs, and dilemmas are not limited to one geographic location or even to one class of people. They are universal and unavoidable. The problem of scarcity—properly considered as the perpetual state of desiring things we don't have, including time itself—confronts rich and poor, city dweller and rural resident, merchant and monk, male and female, theist and agnostic. These are challenges that persist in all times and places and impact everyone. Simply put, economic constraints are an inescapable fact of life in good times and bad and everything in between. Economic constraints are with us, no matter who we are or when or where we abide.

I suspect it is precisely because so many of the parables draw from the enduring realities of economics and commercial life that they provide lasting lessons. The parables deal with topics at a very practical and personal level, as well as on the more profound and higher plane of moral and spiritual obligation. This book, then, seeks to enhance the higher truths the parables contain by investigating the more practical ends of economics, commerce, and business ethics that can be overlooked. In other words, my attempt here is to discern, in the midst of the mundane, the transcendent implications.

It is important to understand at the outset that by economics, I do not mean only buying and selling, much less mere mathematics. I intend more fundamentally the discipline that elucidates the implications of scarcity in the material world: the entire complex nature of exchange, trade, and human action. In particular, I am intrigued by how the economic and commercial perspective can more unfold for us the deeper moral and theoretical implications of Jesus' teaching.

It is not my intention here to derive an economic theory or theology, much less an ideology, from the parables. In point of fact, economics as a scientific or intellectual discipline did not even exist in Jesus' time. Thus, to attribute specific economic policies to the Savior would be anachronistic, even if what is true about economics now was similarly true in the first century. My effort is, instead, to detect the universal economic assumptions at play within the stories themselves, while at the same time acknowledging that these assumptions are not themselves the core intent, moral, or goal of the parable, and that, from time to time, Jesus turns such assumptions on their head to make his point.

A good bit of my public intellectual life has been engaged with economic policy and its consequences, especially the moral consequences of economic decision-making. At the same time, I have always been involved in full-time pastoral work, so my underlying motive for writing this book might be described as an effort at integration or even translation. I wish to show how an economically informed person might approach the parables in a reasonable and sensible way. At any rate, over the years I have detected distinctive points on which my respective fields of endeavor inform each other.

It is obvious that the parables have an economic dimension. Indeed, how would it be possible to speak about the details of human life without reference to the economic? In a sense, then, the continuing relevance of the parables is not all that remarkable because in many ways everyday life is unchanged in essentials. Lessons drawn from commercial life—from how we go about acquiring food, clothing, and housing; how we manage money; how we deal with various social classes; how we buy, and how and what we sell; where we work; how we treat our bosses and employees—still make all the sense in the world. And these are all themes Jesus deals with. To put it simply: Jesus is posing to us the question of how we can derive transcendent lessons from the context of our everyday lives.

The lessons that Jesus sought to convey may be clear at the theological level, and still their application may not be as clear. It would be a mistake to think that these lessons are fixed, simplistic, or static. They can be debated, developed, and applied variously in different circumstances. And not to examine their connections to the economic realities of our lives, I suggest, is to leave our understanding of the parables thinner, less direct, and less relevant and accessible.

Politics necessarily enters into this question, because government, ideology, and civic culture have a profound and increasingly pervasive interest in the management of economic questions today. In writing about the political economy of the parables, I am prepared for the criticism that I am "politicizing" Jesus' teachings, and the potential for this criticism remains clearly before me as I write, but from the outset I proceed with the explicit intention to avoid any such temptation on my part. I certainly hope to correct the politicization of the Scriptures that I have come across over the years, but is it not the contemporary state that has politicized virtually the whole of commercial culture—indeed all of culture? In the time of Jesus, culture was touched more by Roman colonization and the attendant taxation associated with it. Jesus was able to draw universally applicable stories from the commercial life of his day precisely because it was so relatively free of politics and of any detailed regulatory apparatus, compared to today.

Economic structures today are vastly different. Trade is international. Productivity is vastly increased. A complex and global capital structure prevails. Stock markets exist in nearly every country. Modern man has a much higher standard of living than even the elite of Jesus' time.

At the same time, we need to guard against the impression that Jesus came up with these examples to recommend some particular political system or to promote some ideal economic policy. Joachim Jeremias, in his landmark 1966 study, demonstrated that the parables were drawn from the real-life experience that would have been known and understood by the people who heard them in Jesus' time.[8] They were not purely literary constructions. They were not invented to lay down maxims. They are not myth.[9]

Instead, the parables are concerned with life conflicts and difficulties familiar to anyone. They addressed the situation of the moment; they are well-chosen anecdotes simply because these moments keep repeating themselves, all the way to our own times.

The parables I have selected to discuss are chosen because they contain some obvious economic dimension and reveal a great deal about both the way we live and the way we *ought* to live. They are as contemporary as any modern manual on business ethics, and I have no hesitation in predicting that they will long outlast them all.

Even as we look more carefully at the stories themselves and all their economic details, we can never lose sight of the larger purpose in the parables, which is not merely to teach practical aspects of life management but to illumine a fundamental relationship between our lives in all the contingencies of the material world and the good news that Jesus brought into the world—and how this reveals the very mind and intention of God.[10]

We seek transcendent truth in our reflections on the natural order. Facts alone do not satisfy human longing; rather, it is the meaning behind those facts that people seek. Grasping the relationship between skill and devotion can enhance the meaning of our temporal existence, as we contemplate it down to its roots, in all of its messy contingency, so as to glimpse our destiny from our origin: one creator, one truth, one reality whether in time or in eternity.

CHAPTER 1

The Hidden Treasure

"Again, the kingdom of heaven is like unto treasure hid in a field; the which when a man hath found, he hideth, and for joy thereof goeth and selleth all that he hath, and buyeth that field." (Matthew 13:44)

Before us is a lesson in values.

Over time, Jesus' parables have been given various titles, and this one, which is communicated privately to the disciples and not before the multitudes, as was often the case, is often called the Parable of the Hidden Treasure.

The heart of the lesson is clearly the priority of the kingdom of God and urgency of attaining it, no matter how great the sacrifice. Having been discovered, the treasure seizes readers' attention and draws them in, so that they are willing to surrender their present path and seek out a new path instead. The discovery of the treasure is life-altering. There is something in this treasure that captivates the heart and demands relinquishment of all other loves, rendering its discoverer willing to make himself vulnerable so as to obtain something of greater value. What we value and the extent to which we make choices based on those values is the key challenge of the parable. And speculating or looking about us very often enables us to see things that might be obscure or indistinct.

What is the treasure in the parable? It is often imagined to be a chest of gold or purse of precious stones. And why is it hidden? Did the original owner, perhaps generations ago, hide it for fear of war, or famine, or some other disaster?[1] Such a thing would not have been unusual in a society accustomed to invasion and flight. Did the owner forget where he left it? Did he die before telling anyone of its location? Of course this is all surmise, yet it aids our imagination to the extent that it enhances our appreciation of the parable's application. The economic point (which points to a deeper moral truth), is that the treasure was stored there for safekeeping because of uncertainty about the future, possibly because of a reliable calculation or else a mere rumor that the treasure was not safe. Burying treasure in the ground is a very good way of hiding it, with much precedent.

The treasure remains buried until someone finds it. It is easy to imagine people's having walked directly on top of the ground where it lay for decades, leaving it undiscovered. Our discoverer, however, sees its value and gladly parts with everything else he owns in order to buy the land from the current owner and take possession of his treasure. In this one of a series of short parables in Matthew's Gospel we are never told how specifically he happened to find it. He may have discovered it while tilling the ground as an employee or a tenant of the owner, or while he was just out exploring. He may literally have fallen over it. Again, this is just speculation.

Treasure is often a metaphor for wisdom, especially in Scripture. "Receive my instruction, and not silver; and knowledge rather than choice gold," says Proverbs 8:10–11. "For wisdom is better than rubies; and all the things that may be desired are not to be compared to it." One way to secure wealth or resources in the ancient world was to hide them for fear of theft or confiscation. In a similar way, some might think to preserve the treasure of wisdom and of the potential of redemption from a world not safe for truth, or from a culture that might contaminate it. Such a culture, or such people, might not be considered worthy of having a treasure shared with them, thus the admonition: "neither cast ye your pearls before swine, lest they trample them under their feet, and turn again and rend you" (Matthew 7:6), explaining why the parables might be hidden from some but entrusted to others. The treasure has to be *sought* through discovery and effort.

The case of a valuable commodity's being left fallow in a field, not claimed by anyone, presents a buying opportunity. The question then presents itself as to whether the buyer of the field in question has the moral obligation to reveal to its owner that there is a treasure hidden in the field. The parable does not address this particular point (as interesting as it is). Surely the potential buyer is entitled to tell all he knows. But the primary obligation rests with the owner of the property to know the real value of his own property. The one who discovered the treasure is to be congratulated for seeing the opportunity to profit because he sees value where others do not.

This situation may appear as a great moral dilemma, yet it occurs every day in the exchange of goods and services. For example, retailers observe open lots of land that no one seems to place much value on. They see them as places of great potential, where they can bring goods and services and offer them to others. In effect, they see treasure. Does this mean that the owner of the land does not see the future treasure? Perhaps, but not necessarily. The first thing that comes to the mind of the owner is that selling his land to the retailer is an economic advantage. Both parties come out ahead in the exchange, at least from their individual perspectives, which are, of course, the only perspectives they can have.

Another analogy here would be a seller with an old car—a "junker"— with a price tag of $500. Let's say a connoisseur of automobiles comes

The Hidden Treasure, print, after John Everett Millais, engraved and printed by the Dalziel Brothers. *Metropolitan Museum of Art*

along and notices that it is potentially a rare antique worth $50,000. The car is still sold for $500—1 percent of its future market value. The buyer with the knowledge of cars is very much like an entrepreneur in a market, willing to take a risk that the market will bear him out. There is no fraud here, and both benefit from the exchange. If you think about it, in every economic exchange where people are free to accept or reject an offer, both parties are convinced that they got the best deal at the time of the deal.

As to the common assumption that the vendor is taking advantage of the seller, that logic would apply to everyone who runs an ice cream stand and takes advantage of the heat of a summer afternoon; or a restaurateur who takes advantage of people's hunger; or a nurse who takes advantage of someone's illness. But in reality, are these all relationships of exploitation—or of service?

The question to ask is whether there is anything shady going on in these situations. That is a moral question, but it is also a question of *valuation*. Another way to look at it is to ask whether goods such as old cars, or food, or health care, or land have intrinsic economic value in themselves, or if people *bring or create value*—a phenomenon that is sometimes seen in economics. What, after all, do we even mean by "economic value"? Oughtn't we to at least consider that the economic value of the thing depends on the one doing the valuation—that is, the one calculating the worth of the thing at the time it is purchased, which is in turn based on perceptions, opportunities, and availability? In reality, the price of anything is established by the valuation of the item in the mind of the purchaser when goods are exchanged, that is in markets. All of this presupposes complete honesty and a total avoidance of deception in the exchange.

One might argue that it would have been a commendable act of courtesy or even charity to reveal to the owner the existence of treasure. Yet the very framing of such an action as etiquette or charity already concedes that it is not a requirement of either justice or morality. To argue otherwise would be to throw suspicion on a wide assortment of exchanges and arrangements we take for granted, and to hinder human progress and betterment. It would impede the overall creation of wealth in every exchange in which the buyer values the thing for sale at a higher value than the one selling it, and necessitate a kind of educational process prior to every sale in order to convince the seller of the higher value of the object.

Obviously, there is nothing inherently unique about the scenarios described above. In all market exchanges, both parties perceive themselves to be getting the better deal, from their own point of view. Both parties believe that they are made better off as a result of the exchange, and, indeed, we can only trust that their perceptions are correct. When you buy milk from the grocery store, you value the milk more than the $2 it took to purchase it, while the store values the $2 more than the milk. And thus the exchange takes place. Were the milk watered down, or if some other act of deception were employed, it would morally and legally invalidate the deal.

To be sure, buyers and sellers bring different assumptions and different values to the bargaining table. Apart from the theological message of this parable, it also shows that commerce can be mutually beneficial even when there exist different assumptions about the value of the item, that is, when buyer and seller approach an exchange with different objectives in mind. Both parties can still benefit. In the real world, asymmetries in information and values are unavoidable and ubiquitous. A decent and moral economic system is one that creates opportunities for mutual advantage. How could it be otherwise? And would we want it to be?

This parable also tells us something about what it means to discover and to create value in a marketplace. As long as the treasure remained uncovered, unused, and unappreciated in the field, it had no social benefit. It might as well not have existed at all, as far as human well-being was concerned. It didn't bring value to the original owner because he either didn't know it was there or had no appreciation for it.

The treasure does not find us; we have to search it out and develop within ourselves the capacity for recognizing it once it has been found. We also have to be willing to sacrifice to gain possession of it and to relinquish other things that hinder our discovery and capture of the treasure.

The one who has found something no longer pursues it. As the saying goes, "How is it that I always find what I am looking for in the last place I search?" It is the one who has yet to make the discovery who searches, the merchant in search of fine pearls.

The parable of the hidden treasure invites us to ponder a number of things. First, there is what we might learn from what I will call the virtue of attentiveness or alertness on the part of the man who discovers the treasure. The habit of vigilance is commended to us in other parables less subtly, but we should not lose sight of it here as well. Then there is the value our discoverer places on his discovery, a value that causes him to reorder all his other values. A third issue arises here, if not directly from the parable itself, still unavoidably flowing from it. We might ask what the man who discovered the treasure intended to do with it. It's clear that he was not going to leave it in the ground, or he would not have bought the property in the first place. He sees the treasure as enriching.

Consider what gives the treasure its value. Here it is important to distinguish the intrinsic or objective moral values given in the natural order from the values that human beings impart to such things such as commodities by subjectively determining the use we have for them by employing our minds, our intelligence, and the concrete circumstances of our own lives and those of our families and loved ones. In this the human mind reflects to some degree the very mind of the Creator, who created the heavens and the earth, all plants and animals, and then the human person, fashioned in his very image and likeness. Our capacity to discover and even create value is an extension of the power of reason that has been given to us in the *imago Dei* in our very nature. God has "put eternity in their hearts" (Ecclesiastes 3:11).[2] In the human person, the will and the act are one and the same, bringing together the interior and exterior aspects of human nature. God has created us as free actors, responsible, self-determining agents.

We see all this on the temporal or external plane, as we witness people who are especially skilled at discovering and creating subjective value for themselves and others. And on this plane, we need to be cautious so as not to entertain feelings of jealousy or envy, which is the will to destroy. The alternative is the cultivation and appreciation of rare creative talent that can uncover benefits for others and society in general. The future is always uncertain, so people who are willing to take responsible and informed risks are precious—all the more so when they risk their own resources.

Yet the parable reveals something higher than the mundane lessons we can draw from commercial life. It points us to a transcendent wisdom beyond the mundane and inspires us to decode the invitation to grace and union with God hidden within our material world, which points us beyond itself. It is the Kingdom of Heaven that we are being pointed to here—that value above all values, the objective, eternal, intrinsic, and supreme good. While this parable is about the subjective and the temporal, it points us beyond those things. Our business dealings, in which we seek to find economic value by employing unused or under-used resources, are not entirely different from our discovery of something so precious and overlooked that pertains not merely to our time, to our transactions—but to eternity—indeed, to our destiny.

The central actor in our parable is described as selling all his possessions "for joy." A sacrifice can enrich, not merely impoverish us. It is this joy, the joy of the Kingdom, that we ought to put the highest value on—to be willing to sell everything we own to obtain.

CHAPTER 2

The Pearl of Great Price

"Again, the kingdom of heaven is like unto a merchant man, seeking goodly pearls: Who, when he had found one pearl of great price, went and sold all that he had, and bought it." (Matthew 13:45–46)

The Parable of the Pearl of Great Price shares some traits with the previous parable, of the Hidden Treasure. Both involve finding something of great value and deciding to give up all one's possessions in order to obtain it. Both parables compel the reader to ask what it is that prompts a person to sell all in order to obtain something of higher value. Both parables, then, illuminate the course of human life, in which we are continually confronted with opportunities to surrender "a bird in the hand" for "two in the bush," as the old saying goes.

The Parable of the Pearl of Great Price draws on the experience of a merchant. In the Vulgate, Jerome translates *emporo*, the Greek word for "merchant" with the Latin *negotiator*, which implies a person who negotiates something, or one who seeks to sell something to someone at a high price and buy something at a low price.[1] It is the person who wants to make the deal, the one who brings things to an agreed-upon conclusion. The parable is so short that we really do not know whether the central actor intends to turn around and sell the pearl or if he is a collector. But he is engaging in the kind of activity that we see taking place on the stock market every instant of every day. It is the ongoing process in every street bazaar around the world. Prices fluctuate based on human valuation, the subjective knowledge of the parties to the trade, and the availability of resources. A great negotiator seeks to find the price, the point of contact, at which exchange can occur, rendering each person who is party to the exchange pleased with its outcome.

The fact that Jesus employs a luxury good as the central image in this text is, of course, not a legitimization of luxury goods in themselves. Nor is it a condemnation of them. It merely reflects the fact that people value different things at different levels. When people with different values come together, they often exchange things they value less for things they value more—rather than remain static or disconnected from one another.

All too many thoughtful Christians see this fact of people coming together to share and exchange values for mutual benefit as morally suspicious. Some have the impression that charity and commerce, or the practice of faith and the practice of economic exchange, are always antithetical. It is curious that the necessary and ubiquitous experience of merchants and customers prompts such a negative view. Such believers are often prone to assume that the Christian should adopt a perspective that seeks to shun, or render spiritually irrelevant, the actions of a market economy because somehow, rather than being based on love and the common good, business is inevitably animated by selfishness and greed, despite our dependence on such activities. But this concern is not expressed in this parable.

While admittedly it is not the point of the parable to teach us about the importance of trade, it remains difficult for me to see, from the point of view of this and Jesus' other parables, how the wholesale rejection of trade, negotiation, and business has gained such traction among Christians. The parables draw on themes from commerce to make broader moral points about the goal of our lives, our relationships with one another, and even our relationship with God so often that it is hard to see how commerce is evil. This is not to reduce the "economics of the Kingdom" or what theologians have called the "economy of salvation" to the economics of life in general. Nevertheless, ordinary, mundane economics, which I am referring to here, remains a sphere worthy of contemplation and reflection, as we see Jesus engage in these kinds of stories so often.

It goes without saying that the world of two thousand years ago was a world unlike the one most of us know today, where so many more families are able to live in decent homes and shop in fabulously well-stocked stores, which not only would have been unaffordable for most people then, but didn't even exist. For most of human history, life was a struggle for basic necessities like food and shelter, which meant that economic struggles took up the largest part of people's lives. If reflecting on God, or on the challenge of the Kingdom of God, was ever going to be a possibility, it would have to have been done from within this human reality—as Jesus does in this parable, and so many others.

Today, things are different. Cultural themes unite us—like sports or movies—whereas the unifying force in the ancient world was the struggle to survive by obtaining the essentials of life: shelter, clothing, food, and health. In seeking to meet people where they were, Jesus drew on themes that were very familiar to these people, which inevitably meant themes involving commercial life. Were Jesus offering parables today, he might, like many modern preachers, employ analogies or metaphors from sports or entertainment—not to endorse every soccer match or TV series, but to draw people in and point to the Kingdom.

The Pearl of Great Price, print, after John Everett Millais, engraved and printed by the Dalziel Brothers. *Metropolitan Museum of Art*

In many modern liturgical calendars, the cycle of Gospel readings will eventually present all of the parables of Jesus, and the Pearl of Great Price is profoundly striking each time. It is one of eight short parables in Matthew chapter 13, and the whole of it is a mere two sentences long.

This parable, along with numerous others, invites us to contemplate our actions, including buying and selling—actions that many philosophers, from the ancient world right on up to our own day, have thought of as degrading. Jesus, in contrast, uses trade as a means of gaining insight into those actions so as to raise our eyes to the highest of all values: the Kingdom of Heaven. Admittedly, it is a metaphor that is being employed, yet it is intriguing that Jesus would choose this particular metaphor. The cost of discipleship, according to Jesus, is to surrender everything in life, indeed, life itself, in order to take up one's cross and follow (Matthew 16:24).

A pearl is hardly an essential purchase. It is not something to eat. Unlike clothing, it serves no utilitarian function. It was and remains a luxury good, prized as such in the ancient world just as it is today. Obtaining pearls was not easy. In the ancient world, they could not be manufactured; they had to be discovered. The most prized of these were perfectly round in form and translucent in color.[2]

Illustrating how valuable pearls were considered to be, Pliny the Elder describes how Cleopatra, bent on impressing Antony with her opulence, once dissolved a pearl valued at one hundred thousand gold pieces in vinegar and drank it in front of him. Today this would be the equivalent of about a half million dollars. A memorable first date, no doubt.[3]

The pearl was a luxury good and is presented without condemnation in the parable. Instead, Jesus portrays the merchant as wise for having his priorities right in selling what must have been a substantial amount of property in order to obtain it. What might be seen as a pointless material good, may be seen by others as something wonderful, even a reflection of the beauty of Creation itself. People's perspectives, and thus the value they place on objects, differ.

Consider, too, that a pearl is rather small and seemingly insignificant. Its value can only be fully discerned by connoisseurs who appreciate the fineness and uniqueness it possesses. To see the qualities of a fine pearl requires knowledge, expertise, and even mastery. We do indeed need eyes to see and ears to hear what is right in front of us.

Rhetoricians, homilists, and story-tellers frequently hold up merchants to moral scorn, making them examples—object lessons of superficiality and greed. And certainly, the real-life actions of many merchants have provided an abundance of fodder. But in this parable a merchant is presented as an honorable person who possesses special insight and sophistication, as someone who acts in a way that is wise, prudent, good, virtuous, and even courageous. Jesus portrays him as a hero instead of a villain. This merchant is someone who has his priorities in line.

It is worth staying with the term merchant for a bit—a term usually indicating one who sells goods. Indeed, this merchant does sell his goods in order to buy the pearl of supreme value. But we can detect something deeper in this merchant as well: this is a person who discovers something of high value and is willing to take great risks to obtain it. The parable does not portray the merchant as someone who merely pushes a cart and collects cash. He is a negotiator.

The negotiator may be seen as a sort of peacemaker, in the sense that he arranges terms so that every party to the deal achieves a benefit.

Again, the Latin translation of the parable is helpful in deepening our appreciation for the role this merchant or negotiator is playing: the words employed here for "found one" is "*inventa una.*" *Inventa* is, of course, the root of our term invent, which means to bring into being something that did not previously exist. Of course, this merchant does not literally create the pearl *ex nihilo*, but he does invent or create value that did not previously exist—both by his knowledge of the general value of pearls of this quality and by his discovery of its availability. It is in this sense that he brings value into being where it did not previously exist. The negotiator observes the possibility that a pearl could be of enormous value and then risks all he owns to obtain it.

We describe a negotiator who invents or discovers value as an entrepreneur—a revealing word implying growth. Here speakers of English have taken over the French word to describe a person who creates or starts a new project, or one who takes on a new opportunity or venture, incurring risks in the market to see it to fruition.

We might note that in this parable the entrepreneur does not find the pearl inside an oyster on a beach, which is where one usually discovers pearls. Instead, he finds it in the market, where it is already owned by someone, and purchases it. This requires powers of insight (to see the value of the pearl when others have overlooked it) and persuasion (to bring about the agreement). Jesus' utilization of this scenario in relation to the Kingdom of Heaven is an example of what I alluded to earlier—an insight into the Kingdom drawn from the habits and processes of business.

Throughout my life I have often come across the sentiment which expresses in one way or another a moral suspicion of private ownership as an expression of greed while favoring some sort of collective ownership which is considered more generous or socially oriented. The lesson of this parable emerges only when the arrangement allows for what is owned privately to be priced and sold on the marketplace to other potential owners. Again, I have no desire to insert a meaning into this parable that is not the intention of Jesus to teach, nor do I believe Jesus is specifically trying to make an economic point. Rather, Jesus assumes the insights that come from economic reality, and so enables us to derive some insight from the principles and assumptions the parable already contains. We can then apply that insight to the modern context.

To reiterate, this parable is not a lesson in pricing theory; we are dealing here in metaphors. The point Jesus is making is that the Kingdom of Heaven comes at a *price*—he is speaking to us of the overall notion of cost and valuation, only one dimension of which is economic. The lesson is that we must surrender all temporal attachments, incurring some "costs" so as to attain something of infinitely greater value. And this will require of us the same kind of discernment, willingness to risk, and trust that our judgement of the risk is appropriate to the goal that the purchaser of the pearl exhibits. In a sense, we have to negotiate our way through all the competing values and other tugs at our hearts that the alternatives offer. In the life of Jesus, we see one who paid the ultimate price of his life so as to open up eternal life for all the faithful. My point is that unless we speak in some sense of a "price" which also implies a "cost," we are left with a much less substantial appreciation of the "value" of the Kingdom of God. At the very least, the language of economics can point our gaze upward, beyond the material world.

The substructure of the commercial exchange enables us to understand the transcendent lesson at a deeper level. So to see the buying and selling characteristic of merchants and entrepreneurs as merely something evil will encumber our minds and cause us to miss the essential meaning of this parable.

If we understand the proper role of commercial activity and appreciate profits, losses, and trading as part of the limited structure of this world, our insight into this and other parables will be enhanced.

To understand markets, to work within their contingencies, and to discover ways in which these temporal matters throw light on the Christian truths by which we can sharpen our vocations as spiritual entrepreneurs, so to speak, are all things that will enable us to see that, in the end, what is of ultimate value, and what gives sense and meaning to all valuation, comes from God and must be directed back toward God. Unless we are prepared to surrender all, perhaps even incurring risk in the process, when that opportunity presents itself to us, we may never obtain that thing of higher, indeed infinite, value. All of this, of course, requires faith in an end that we do not presently see.

There is nothing of greater value in this world than to be at one with God both temporally and eternally, that is, to embrace the truth in all its fullness. To see and understand this requires an insight not terribly different from that of an entrepreneur. To obtain such insight means to be willing to engage in a kind of exchange whereby we give up what we previously thought was valuable in order to obtain something even more wonderful.

A Pearl of Great Price indeed.

CHAPTER 3

The Sower

"And he spake many things unto them in parables, saying, Behold, a sower went forth to sow; and when he sowed, some seeds fell by the way side, and the fowls came and devoured them up: Some fell upon stony places, where they had not much earth: and forthwith they sprung up, because they had no deepness of earth: And when the sun was up, they were scorched; and because they had no root, they withered away. And some fell among thorns; and the thorns sprung up, and choked them: But other fell into good ground, and brought forth fruit, some an hundredfold, some sixtyfold, some thirtyfold. Who hath ears to hear, let him hear." (Matthew 13:3–9)

N ot every parable contains an explanation of its meaning, but the Parable of the Sower does. Jesus tells us that this parable refers to the response to the Word of God. The sower is a preacher, and the seeds are truth.[1] Here, as so often in Scripture, the Kingdom of Heaven is compared to a harvest.[2]

The lesson here is one about receptivity, communicated through the metaphor of land; it is a lesson about the varied reactions of people, some of whom are well disposed for the Kingdom of Heaven and some of whom are not. Of course the ground cannot make itself receptive to the seed. But the land represents people here. For some, the Word is accepted but not appropriated, and so their faith withers. For others, the Word is accepted, but only superficially, and when difficulties arise the Word is discarded or betrayed. There are varying degrees of understanding and tenacity, but in only one case in this parable does the faith produce spectacular growth, and that is when it is permitted to penetrate deeply.

To appreciate the meaning of the parable requires understanding of the agricultural metaphor—an understanding that would have been much more broadly achieved at a time when a large majority of the population provided for themselves directly through the industry of agriculture. The story addresses many questions. We might ask whether nature is our friend or our enemy. To what extent must our minds be engaged in order to bring forth productivity, in order to cultivate the land (or ourselves) so as to be more receptive? We might even have to ask a question so often raised today about the abuse of the land, about abuse or neglect that makes land less receptive and productive.

Just as a crop of wheat is not produced in a day—it requires preparation, cultivation, and waiting—so too can we anticipate that the Kingdom of God will not appear in its fullness all at once. Preparatory work and patience are needed. It is more like a tiny seed that grows systematically and relentlessly, but only under the right conditions.

A seed cannot flourish under just any conditions, as every farmer knows. It can be eaten by birds, choked out by weeds, find no soil in which to grow, or be scorched by the sun. Both interior and exterior factors may play a role. What constitutes good ground? This is the critical question, on which economics can shed some light. Good soil—meaning productive soil that is hospitable to fruitfulness—is cultivated soil. Effort is put into this cultivation, and to be productive this effort requires a knowledge of the nutritional needs of each specific crop. Certainly, in the regions of the world in which these parables were first heard, most ground was not good ground in its natural state. It was too arid, too naturally dry. In order for this land to be suitable to support growth, it had to be tilled and prepared well. Rocks had to be removed and thorns pulled up. The soil had to be amended by watering, and the crops guarded and protected from weeds and animal pests.

Preparing the ground required human hands directed by human intelligence. Skill, study, experience, and good management were all necessary. What is at play here is not only the legitimacy and dignity of human work but also its necessity. Contrary to some contemporary sentiments, it is the very manipulation—in the truest meaning of the word, that is "fashioning with one's hands"—of the natural environment that makes an otherwise barren plot fruitful. Effort must be applied to the soil. One modern fashion, indeed prejudice, would have us think that a pristine environment untouched by humanity is somehow morally superior.

And yet impediments that prevent people from cultivating nature so often end up rendering nature unproductive. And to what end? If the land is valued only for the sake of sight-seeing and beauty, the impediments to its cultivation are understandable enough, though even in these contexts the land will require some kind of maintenance and care. But when limitations on human cultivation of the land are undertaken out of the mistaken belief that untilled land is somehow morally preferable to land that has been worked or cultivated, problems arise. The jungle is not always to be preferred to the garden.

For those who hold to a kind of environmentalist religion, Jesus' parable will be incomprehensible. A sower can only prepare the

New Testament Illustrations, The Sower by Johann Eck. *British Museum*

ground if he is its lawful owner or under contract by its lawful owner to do the work. This assures that the land and its increasing value will be protected from invasion, looting, or expropriation.

Let me be clear: I am not asserting that the intention of the parable is to give a seminar on the legitimacy of private ownership. Not even the eighth commandment's prohibition on theft has that purpose, though it does presume private ownership. Economics is not the point either of the commandments or of the parables. Private ownership is simply assumed as part of the structure of the story, and indeed as a demand of human nature in its temporal reality. But because this and other similar stories would not make much sense without postulating private property, I think it is a useful exercise to examine it. That effort will enhance our appreciation for the drama of the parables. To my mind, it is remarkable that so essential an institution has come under severe attack and skepticism through the centuries, most especially in the name of religion. Even the metaphor of a garden, something that is ordinarily made possible by private property, raises the question of flourishing—or, as it is called in the field of economics, profit. A lack of ownership often results in chaos (the jungle replaces the garden) when people are no longer able to place value on the land. Public ownership is less productive to the extent that it discourages anyone from taking responsibility for the land. Forced collective ownership (and for that matter, even voluntary collective ownership) can promote a culture of "free riding." Since no one person is responsible for maintenance, everyone leaves it to someone else to follow through on tasks. Think of the typical condition of a public bathroom. This has been called "the tragedy of the commons."

Saint Thomas Aquinas provides us with an excellent explanation of this point:

Man has a twofold competence in relation to material things. The first is the title to care for and distribute the earth's resources. Understood in this way, it is not merely legitimate for a man to possess things as his own, it is even necessary for human life, and this for three reasons. First, because each person takes more trouble to care for something that is his sole responsibility than what is held in common or by many—for in such a case each individual shirks the work and leaves the responsibility to somebody else, which is what happens when too many officials are involved. Second, because human affairs are more efficiently organized if each person has his own responsibility to discharge; there would be chaos if everybody cared for everything. Third, because men live together in greater peace where everyone is content with his task.[3]

In order to reap the benefits of what is planted, the property needs someone who takes responsibility for it. This person needs to control the environment in a way that is most conducive to productivity and eventual harvest. This may be either the owner, or someone hired and directed to act in the owner's interest, who might even care for the land with greater knowledge and precision than the owner.

The parable teaches us a great deal about the land's reception of the seed: Under the right conditions—when the seed is in effect invested in the right environment prepared by human hands, that is, cultivated, it can return anywhere from thirty to one hundred times what was sown. A single seed can not only become a crop; it can provide the basis for further growth and prosperity.

This imagery is clearly an allegory for evangelization, the increase of faith, and the universal offer of redemption. Relationship with God is offered without limit to anyone who embraces it because

God never runs out of love. The concept of profit, the gain from economic activity that results from resources well used, illuminates the soteriological message, bringing it closer to us and making it more comprehensible to people in the everyday world. How is profit like evangelization? Both involve being fruitful in accomplishing what one has set out to do.

Think for a moment of what it means to make a profit. It is to achieve a gain, rather than a loss, from an economic activity. Profits are often considered morally suspect, sometimes for the same reasons that evangelization is seen as suspect, to the extent that it can be exploitative in its disregard for human dignity. But in a strict sense, to profit only means to avoid making a loss. In trade, it is valuable to discover tangible evidence that one's activities have netted a gain for everyone by rendering a benefit over a previous circumstance. To profit is to produce a harvest that is worth more than the effort that went into planting it. Put simply, profit is "an indication that a business is functioning well."[4]

In any economic exchange, two different things must be harmonized. The first is the subjective value to the consumer: what he or she sees as desirable, useful, or needed. This is the level of utility— an important and undeniable economic truth. This is parallel to the dynamic that comes into play when the message of Christ is proposed to someone who then comes to see that his needs are met by an acceptance of the message.

This second reality comes into play simultaneously with the first. The one doing the trading is a human person, and while the economic truth about human conditions is true, it is not the whole truth. Something more needs to be taken into consideration, something that encompasses a fuller understanding of the human person. To reiterate: the subjective dimension is true and useful for calculation; but it is not the whole truth about who the human person is.

There is a psychological profit associated with every economic action. People trade with one another with the expectation that they will be better off than before they engaged. Otherwise, why trade in the first place? It is the same with investing—of which the cultivation of a field might be considered an example. All of us want to back efforts that are successful, and profitability is an indication of that. It is true of a market economy generally as it is of the cultivating of a field. Likewise, efforts of evangelization contain the hope of spiritual profitability, as we see in Jesus' metaphor: "The harvest truly is plenteous, but the labourers are few; Pray ye therefore the Lord of the harvest, that he will send forth labourers into his harvest" (Matthew 9:37–38). This creative dynamic, when cultivated into a habit, can encourage a tendency to reward or affirm decisions that are consistent with the prudent use of resources and accomplishing goals set forth. To the extent to which humans depend on abundance to live better, such a dynamic can help to bring about this abundance.

In a market economy (as opposed to, say, a kleptocracy) the only way that high profits can come about is when a seller provides products or services that the public wants to purchase, at prices that they find attractive. This does not mean that the products the public chooses will always be the best ones, or the free market itself encourages virtue. Market exchange turns on the *subjective* value that a consumer places on a product, not on the objective values that are better called virtues. The critical task of forming character and conscience rests primarily with parents in the home, spiritual directors and guides, and a host of other authorities, not on economic institutions as such.

Free markets can allow people to obtain the goods and services they desire, whether their desires are for real or illusory goods. Other institutions are necessary to channel their desires toward what is truly good, by providing moral habituation to virtue. The erroneous belief that the market is sufficient to resolve every problem of humanity is the "neo-liberal dogma" that would put everything up for sale.[5]

We must keep in mind that what is reflected on the level of economics are only subjective values, not virtues. Entrepreneurs profit to the extent that they serve the public, in the sense of fulfilling each consumer's subjective desires, whether those desires are virtuous or vicious. But when people's subjective tastes are elevated, the fulfillment of their desires can help to form a more broadly virtuous culture in environments where enterprise thrives and the products they want are produced in abundance.

Aside from artists, entrepreneurs are the most obvious examples of persons who use the creative talents entrusted to them by the Creator for the authentic good of others. In a market economy, others can also exercise the virtue of enterprise and creativity in numerous ways. Workers can discover better ways to accomplish tasks, and owners and employers will be wise to be open to their suggestions, always attentive to better alternatives. The flexibility to be able to change jobs and seek out new opportunities more suitable or receptive to these insights provides an institutional assurance that those with new ideas and talents can discover the best ways and circumstances to place them at the disposal of others, making contributions to the overall well-being of society by putting those ideas and talents at the service of others.

In some sense, we are all sowers of seeds and tillers of soil. To the extent that we live out our respective vocations diligently, we may hope to see positive results, what we might call "productivity." The Parable of the Sower does not speak of the *limits* to growth but rather of the *potential* for growth. The world of the parables is not a world of scarcity, but a world where there is the promise of abundance under the right conditions.

Almost everyone says they favor growing economies and prosperity. But far too little attention is paid to the conditions that actually and concretely make prosperity possible. Not all institutional settings equally favor economic growth. Economies cannot grow if they are choked by the thorns of regulations and confiscatory taxes. They cannot grow if the environment in which they are situated does not contain the proper elements that will protect, encourage, and sustain productivity. The rocks in this parable can be seen as a metaphor for a fully controlled economy, with a static, immovable collection of obstructions that permit little possibility for development, productivity, or creativity, thus closing off growth, placing arduous and sometimes immovable obstacles in the path to creativity. Whatever ingenuity is attempted immediately dies because there is no soil in which it is permitted to grow, no room for it to blossom.

Economic awareness enables us to see how this parable reinforces the practical and moral legitimacy of private property, human achievement, and economic growth. After all, we all sow seeds in this world that we hope will yield in abundance. Every action we take, even if mistaken, is performed with the hope of making a situation or condition better—to diminish dis-ease in some fashion. The soil must be receptive in order to achieve this purpose. The core lesson of the Parable of the Sower relates to the receptivity of the human heart to the offer of grace, a willingness to listen, to learn, and to receive. The desire to embrace truth when we find it is the challenge, and it is vital to know what enables or disables that capacity.

Chapter 4

The Laborers in the Vineyard

"For the kingdom of heaven is like unto a man that is an householder, which went out early in the morning to hire labourers into his vineyard. And when he had agreed with the labourers for a penny a day, he sent them into his vineyard. And he went out about the third hour, and saw others standing idle in the marketplace, And said unto them; Go ye also into the vineyard, and whatsoever is right I will give you. And they went their way. Again he went out about the sixth and ninth hour, and did likewise. And about the eleventh hour he went out, and found others standing idle, and saith unto them, Why stand ye here all the day idle? They say unto him, Because no man hath hired us. He saith unto them, Go ye also into the vineyard; and whatsoever is right, that shall ye receive. So when even was come, the lord of the vineyard saith unto his steward, Call the labourers, and give them their hire, beginning from the last unto the first. And when they came that were hired about the eleventh hour, they received every man a penny. But when the first came, they supposed that they should have received more; and they likewise received every man a penny. And when they had received it, they murmured against the goodman of the house, saying, These last have wrought but one hour, and thou hast made them equal unto us, which have borne the burden and heat of the day. But he answered one of them, and said, Friend, I do thee no wrong: didst not thou agree with me for a penny? Take that thine is, and go thy way: I will give unto this last, even as unto thee. Is it not lawful for me to do what I will with mine own? Is thine eye evil, because I am good? So the last shall be first, and the first last." (Matthew 20:1–16)

One marvels at the sustaining power of the parables when reading this teaching. After two thousand years, the drama is still intense. We remain captivated by the story and identify with the characters. The issues in the Parable of the Laborers in the Vineyard continue to confront us today in direct ways. (We can sense the stress of having a crop ready to harvest and needing workers to harvest it, for example, and we all face deadlines of one sort or another.) This gives the story force. This parable illuminates the human choice to accept God's grace, with its attendant rewards. It also shines light on issues related to the justice and fairness of wages in a marketplace and shows how character and the reward of labor are not easily separated. The parable reveals something about the vice of jealousy as well as the virtue of generosity.

This parable contains a hard truth: workers are compensated by mutual agreement. In the whole scope of moral consideration, this may not be the final word, but it is the beginning word. The manner in which the story unfolds conjures up a sympathy for the workers who worked all day and received no more than the workers who came at the last hour. But as we ponder it more deeply, we find ourselves wondering if our sympathy for the workers who labored all day is actually rooted in a kind of resentment against generosity. After all, no one is being defrauded here. Surprised—yes, even disappointed—but not defrauded or treated unjustly. The vineyard owner is right that his high wages for the last workers are a form of charity.

There are countless spiritual and material insights one can extract from the details of this challenging story.

In this story, a landowner needed workers in his vineyard and so offered to pay them a particular wage, one *denarius*, which, according to the best scholarship, was a subsistence wage and no more.[1]

While no one was forced to work and everyone came of his own volition, there would nonetheless be plenty of room for charity here. A sufficient number of laborers showed up to start the workday, but halfway through the morning the vineyard owner realized that there weren't sufficient workers to complete the job. This presented the potential catastrophe of a substantial part of the harvest's being lost because of a shortage of workers.

Noting the labor shortage and being an entrepreneur, the vineyard owner went to town and noticed a number of able-bodied men sitting around doing nothing. He asked them why they were idle, and they answered that nobody had offered them work. He hired them, but told them that the pay would depend on how well they did. They agreed. All throughout the day, he did the same, rounding up workers anywhere he could find them. Eventually, he had enough to complete the job by the end of the workday.

He was jubilant that the job was done, and we can imagine that he felt especially generous as the sun began to set. His generosity was on display at pay time. He paid the last men to arrive at the vineyard their wages, which happened to be the same amount he had promised the people who got there first. They must have been

Parable of the Workers in the Vineyard by Jan Luyken. *Rijksmuseum*

very pleased. He did the same for all the others as well, paying everyone for a full day's work. Then he came to the first people hired, and it turned out that, by now, they fully expected that they would get more. But to their surprise they received exactly what they were promised, and no more than those who had worked only a short time. The order of payment makes an intentional point.

They did what anyone would do in a market: they complained to the landowner himself. And the landowner responded with three extremely salient points, one having to do with contracts, the second centering on legality, and the third having to do with morality.

First, he pointed out that this was not a matter of justice, but of subjective perspective, since he had met the terms of the specified contract. That is the definition of justice: giving to each his due. The workers had the opportunity to accept or reject the contract at the outset, and they accepted. Thus, as the landowner rightly pointed out, their complaint was not about their own paycheck but the paychecks of others. He then addressed the question of whether he had the right to pay the others whatever he wanted to pay them. The answer is yes, since, as he so clearly put it, he had the right to do what he wanted with his own money: "Is it not lawful for me to do what I will with mine own?" If you think about this, it is simply an appeal to common sense, and it must have been frustrating to those first workers.

Finally, and most penetratingly, he focused on the moral case. In paying the people who came later the same wage for less work, he was really engaging in an act of generosity. He might have done this to encourage them to come back and work for him at a later date. Or perhaps he was engaging in pure charity because he felt they needed the money. It might have just been his reaction to the abundant harvest. In any case, even if we are unwilling to celebrate the good fortune of others, we surely have no right to condemn it and begrudge them! The morally astute landowner in effect asks them if they are envious of his generosity when he says: "Is thine eye evil, because I am good?" He then dismisses everyone.

This parable teaches us something of God's gratuity in the way he treats those who come to him at the last possible moment. The Good Thief on the cross comes to mind. Salvation is offered to all, regardless of tribe, class, or other consideration, whether they live holy lives or repent only minutes before death. This is the essence of grace: it is unearned; it cannot be demanded as a right. Rather, it comes as a gift. Just as by the day's end all available workers were given the opportunity to come to the vineyard, so too is everyone invited to the kingdom of God. It is an invitation that must be accepted, just as grace is accepted. The "payment" for accepting grace is salvation. All who come receive. The primary purpose of the story is to reveal this truth in a manner that draws on practical experience.

But we can also discern the practical economic import of the story as well. First, we learn that in an economy with ownership and wages there really is no equal pay for equal work—or rather, there does not have to be. What there is, is contracted pay for contracted work. Anything outside of this is discretionary. Certain moral claims may require paying more. Prudence is certainly necessary. And decency might demand a certain realization of non-market wage outcomes. As always, certain cultural norms or customs may apply. It is a good thing that every worker should be free to make a contract for whatever terms of employment he deems appropriate for himself, and that every employer be free to make any offer he deems sustainable for his business. After that, the legal obligation of both the worker and the employer is to be faithful to the terms of the contract. The worker may choose to work longer hours, just as the owner may choose to pay additional wages to latecomers. But human beings are more than contractors and contracted. Without this first step however, which reveals what the true costs are, the entire enterprise falters. This is the stuff of economics. It does us no good to obscure this reality, even if we may decide to supplement it on account of additional considerations.

Rewards in a market economy are not distributed as Karl Marx imagined them to be. Prices and wages are not determined by the amount of sweat and muscle expended; they are determined by the subjective value of the final product. Putting it another way, it is the value to those who will (or will not) purchase the product that determines the value or price of that product. Economists would say that this value is "imputed back" to all of the factors of production.[2] For example, workers producing outdated computers can't expect the same remuneration as those making the next generation of computers. Why? Because the monetary value of work is related to the market worth of what that work produces—that is, to the subjective value of the product to the one who buys it. And most people are just not going to buy outdated computers. The monetary value of work is not some arbitrary or capricious amount set by the owner or the producer; it is the price set by the consumer.

This isn't because one group works harder than the other group, or is made up of people who are somehow better. It is because they are better able to serve people's needs—as determined by those very people and the value they place on one product over another. That value is reflected in the wages they are paid. The landowner in Jesus' parable was thrilled that his vineyard was harvested completely. One can imagine that it was a bountiful harvest—thanks to the perceptive and determined actions of the landowner. Happy about that, he distributed payment in a generous way. It is the final result—a job well done—that determined the wage. How very much like the market itself, which can even be "generous" to people that most of us wouldn't regard as deserving.

By virtue of the limited material reality in which we live, human beings are dependent on market activities to ensure their survival. Still, because humans are more than material entities, there is also something due to human beings as human persons—something that exceeds the logic of the market.

The person in the best position to determine what the subsistence level is, is the worker himself. Too quick a regulatory fix—either in the labor market or in controlling the price of goods—creates a distortion, making it impossible to know what the real costs are, what a sustainable price or wage is.

The problem of sub-standard wages is a real one. But this real problem is not remedied by ignoring the information that free exchange yields, or pretending it doesn't exist. While our intention would be to provide for the well-being of people, the lack of information will only hinder the prospects for human betterment that prosperity provides.

When businesses promote legislation that will hobble their competitors, they exhibit the very disposition of the first laborers who worked the longest. They are convinced that they should be rewarded at least as well for their labors as others. But in reality—in real life and in real markets, where rivalry and consumer tastes can take unpredictable paths because of human subjectivity—we see that no one has an entitlement to a profit. Enterprise means assuming risks and being willing to suffer a loss when one's best judgment turns out to be less profitable than one hoped.

As Jennifer Roback Morse explains, efforts to correct for the apparent unfairness of the market actually reward envy and make it profitable. Borrowing language from moral theology, she says that regulatory structures and many other forms of political intervention actually provide an "occasion of sin."[3] That phrase is taken from the Act of Contrition, a prayer of sorrow and repentance, and it refers to a situation or an environment that, while itself not sinful, nevertheless puts one in proximity to or on a trajectory toward sin.

It is not wise for recovering alcoholics to hang around bars, where they are merely providing themselves an unnecessary temptation against their sobriety. There is a parallel here with arbitrarily applied economic regulation: this kind of regulation gives business competitors something to use in preference to the difficulty of marketplace competition with other businesses. It places an entire economy on a deleterious and regulatory path moving it closer to the "sin" of economic dislocations and impoverishment.

Commerce itself can and in fact often does reinforce a wide range of traditional and practical virtues. Clean and clear lines of ownership, discernable boundaries of property rights, the enforcement of contracts—all these things discourage theft and encourage peaceful exchange, cooperation, and human solidarity. Vibrant capital markets encourage creativity and long-range planning, even as the system of profit and loss discourages waste and encourages a wise use of resources. Even the existence of interest rates discourages untrammeled consumption and rewards deferred gratification. When we add to all this institutions such as credit reports and other forms of reputation-tracking that encourage meeting one's obligations and keeping promises, we can see the potential for a culture of morality to emerge from the free market naturally, without manipulation.

After all, in order to be practically generous—the virtue so abundantly displayed by the landowner in this parable—it is first necessary to have an abundant harvest, to create superfluous wealth, something that is possible only in a culture that prevents envy and jealousy from institutionalizing themselves and obscuring the information that free exchange makes available. The creation of wealth requires a society that rewards rather than penalizes productivity.

CHAPTER 5

The Rich Fool

"And one of the company said unto him, Master, speak to my brother, that he divide the inheritance with me. And he said unto him, Man, who made me a judge or a divider over you? And he said unto them, Take heed, and beware of covetousness: for a man's life consisteth not in the abundance of the things which he possesseth. And he spake a parable unto them, saying, The ground of a certain rich man brought forth plentifully: And he thought within himself, saying, What shall I do, because I have no room where to bestow my fruits? And he said, This will I do: I will pull down my barns, and build greater; and there will I bestow all my fruits and my goods. And I will say to my soul, Soul, thou hast much goods laid up for many years; take thine ease, eat, drink, and be merry. But God said unto him, Thou fool, this night thy soul shall be required of thee: then whose shall those things be, which thou hast provided? So is he that layeth up treasure for himself, and is not rich toward God." (Luke 12:13–21)

The parable of the Rich Fool comes on the heels of what might initially strike us as an odd request. Jesus is asked to adjudicate a personal family conflict. The younger brother is upset that his older brother is not sharing the inheritance with him. (A similar tension arises in the parable of the Prodigal Son.) Jesus' response is unexpected. Instead of extending the hand of sympathy and settling the familial discord, Jesus upbraids the younger brother for his real motivation—in striking language. He tells the younger brother that it is not his place to act as an arbiter in a legal dispute. He is not there to determine the proper distribution of goods. He sees in the younger brother's request a hidden sin: avarice, greed, covetousness, or miserliness: "And he said unto him, Man, who made me a judge or a divider over you? And he said unto them, Take heed, and beware of covetousness: for a man's life consisteth not in the abundance of the things which he possesseth."

It seems probable that the young man who came to him with the request was taken aback by Jesus' comment, and one can imagine how it must have surprised the crowd as well. It is usual that when someone approaches someone else with deference—as the younger brother did, acknowledging Jesus' wisdom and authority to resolve the matter—the person approached is flattered. But Jesus was not.

Under Jewish law, the first son is set to inherit twice the amount of a younger male sibling.[1] If there are other siblings, the money is further divided, but the eldest still receives twice the amount of the others, each of whom receives the same amount. The math is complicated enough when we are talking about cash. But imagine the problems that arise with in-kind property transfers! In other words, the situation is ripe for litigation and acrimony.

Anyone who has ever been involved in an inheritance dispute knows all too well that they are among the ugliest of all conflicts. In my pastoral work I have encountered family members who preferred

The Parable of the Rich Fool by Ambrosius Francken. *Royal Library of Belgium*

to just walk away and allow their siblings and others to have what they wanted, seeing that as preferable to an all-out familial war. Jesus may be suggesting that this would be a better path than unleashing deeply rooted and long-lasting family hatreds, which often have nothing to do with the inheritance in question, but with deep, complex, unresolved sibling conflicts.

It is not unusual for commentators on this parable to take sides. Is the younger brother being covetous, or is the elder brother being selfish? Would that it were that simple. I have found that there is often plenty of culpability to go around. Of course, both sides claim to be holding the most reasonable and just position. And both become implacable. These kinds of disputes often create unresolvable conflicts that can leave division as the sad and abiding inheritance for a family.

The Parable of the Rich Fool, engraving by Adriaen Collaert after Hans Bol. *National Gallery of Art*

Nor do such dynamics apply only in family matters. Whole societies and nations, undergirded by similar motivations, can find themselves in similarly intractable disputes. Who should own the wealth? How should it be divided or shared? Who should benefit at whose expense? And why? If injustice exists, what should be the resolution? As with the two fighting brothers, there can be no end to such conflicts once they get started. People turn against each other, divided along the lines of social or economic class, race, sex, or religion. Karl Marx understood this well enough to build a revolutionary philosophy out of it.

How often is Christianity called upon to intervene to bring about a more just distribution of the world's goods? That message is a staple in pulpits around the world. It is routinely said that it is the role of

Christianity to take from the rich and give to the poor, to expropriate property owners on behalf of those without, to take from the haves and give to the have-nots (in a kind of Robin Hood economic theology). Contemporary writers like Elizabeth Bruenig and Mathew Schmalz argue that admonitions against making an idol of property or profit bespeak a left-wing bias in the Scriptures, and at least one writer explicitly argues that Jesus was a socialist.[2]

Never mind that arguments like these are largely ahistorical, anachronistic attempts to eisegetically read back into the Scriptures ideologies and economic systems that were developed much later in the history of ideas. I hope it is clear that in this book I have made a conscious effort to eschew any such eisegetical temptation from the opposite point of view.

Here, Jesus confronts a problem for which he could have advocated precisely this kind of redistributionist resolution. But he refuses. Instead, he gives us the key to understanding his message by lifting our vision to a higher level and delivers a short homily on the vices of envy, materialism, and avarice, whether in those who demand or in those who refuse to give. We rarely hear anyone point to the demands of the have-nots as being motivated by greed, and yet the poor, like the rich, can be inspired by ill motives. Indeed, it would be understandable—even if not justifiable—for those lacking resources, precisely because of their great needs, to be tempted to employ illegitimate means of acquiring wealth.

There is another practical factor at play here. Redistribution of wealth can be enormously wasteful of time and resources. It creates no wealth. It only moves around the wealth that has already been created and contains its own costs to perform. Rather than enlarging the overall pie, it merely slices it up, reducing the share of some and enlarging the share of others. There are times when it's a good idea to do this, especially within families. But if the redistribution is orchestrated by officials far removed from the concrete context, or motivated by avarice, or covetousness, or envy, it can be the occasion of sin, all too often promoting violence and injustice.

Oddly enough it was not a biblical commentator but a statesman who offered the most telling corrective to this confusion between Christianity and socialism. Winston Churchill observed that, "the socialism of the Christian era...was based on the idea that 'all mine is yours,' but the Socialism of [today] is based on the idea that 'all yours is mine.'"[3]

It is unclear whether the younger brother who came to Jesus about his inheritance was seeking a definitive ruling, or if he was just asking the Lord to offer a persuasive opinion to his brother. Today, we live in one of the most litigious societies in the history of the world. When something goes wrong in our relations with others, we very often seek a legal remedy rather than any sort of conciliation. What are we looking for when we call lawyers and file lawsuits? Justice? Or are we reaching for some sort of club with which to beat money out of people? Are we seeking to strengthen our position? By failing to look at the ultimate goal and meaning of our existence, we often rob the present moment of a sense of meaning and purpose.

Resolving social tensions by dialogue and mutual respect and understanding is far preferable morally, personally, and even economically. This is why, no doubt, a number of organizations and legal firms now offer things such as "inheritance dispute resolution" to help avoid legal conflicts.[4]

Social peace, reconciliation, and harmony can only emerge in a culture in which people value those things called economic and political advantage.

From time to time, almost all of us have received an invitation informing us that we are eligible to join a class action lawsuit. Perhaps it was a drill you bought at the hardware store, a baby seat, a delayed airline flight, or a refrigerator. Chances are that you had no real problem at all with your purchase. Often in such class action law suits we find that a company has agreed to pay people only as a way to cut its legal losses and avoid further courtroom fights. It would be a good idea for you to examine your motives before joining such a lawsuit. Are you seeking genuine justice, or just money? Again, we need to keep the end, the *telos* before our eyes.

These are legitimate questions that relate to morality and economics. Our society is beset by divisive politics, a torn social fabric, and rampant and wasteful litigation. Tort reform and political reform can help, but the ultimate solution is a cultural reform. Human beings themselves must begin to seek other means of resolving disputes besides legal and political redress, and they must hand on that value to the next generation.

It is noteworthy that Jesus declines the suggestion that he should intervene and act as a litigator or redistributor of property. Instead, he turns his attention to framing the broader priorities by telling a story with some very interesting implications. If the brother or brothers can learn the lesson, perhaps a real resolution is possible. The story is of a man who found a way to wealth, which in turn transformed him. He evidently succumbed to the notion that mere accumulation was his path to happiness. So he plotted to store up things so as to be liberated from all work. Then, in a twist of tragic fate, he died—and all his ambitious plans died with him. The end of the story is rather abrupt, leaving the hearer with a sense of shock, but also, one hopes, with some moral clarity.

On one level, from an economic point of view, the man was making a sensible calculation. A sound economic perspective yields a certain understanding of the truth of a situation. In this case, it is the accumulation of an abundance of wealth to enable the man to retire in security. Jesus' lesson here is not that this economic point is false; it is just that it is not the whole truth.

After all, what is there to show for his efforts? Vast quantities of unconsumed food. Some other things are lacking: good works, heroism, children, memories, or a legacy. In Jesus' telling of the man's story, none of this appears—just a stark finality. In the end there was nothing but produce left to rot. The clear message is that this is not a life to be celebrated, this was not a "full life" even if it was full of things. This is the ultimate anti-materialist parable demonstrating how "you can't take it with you"; it may even be the origin of the phrase itself. Yet there is a way to, in effect, "take it with you." Saint Ambrose tells us how "Virtue is the companion of the dead. Mercy alone follows us, and mercy alone gains abodes for the departed."[5] In the end, this man did not possess too much; he possessed *too little*.

Do we learn from this parable that we should not plan for the future? Hardly. People who do not plan for the future are rightly seen as frivolous and irresponsible elsewhere in the parables of Jesus, such as the Parables of the Wise and Foolish Virgins (Matthew 25:1–13), the Wise and Foolish Builders (Matthew 7:24–27; Luke 6:46–49), and the Unjust (but shrewd) Steward (Luke 16:1-13). We do well to conserve resources, not to be spendthrifts, to save and not spend all our earnings. Frugality is also a virtue. To behave in our economic lives as if there were no tomorrow would be to act irrationally and irresponsibly, both for ourselves and for our loved ones. The chances are we will not die tomorrow, and to act as though we will would be to leave many important things undone. If it is foolish to be miserly and selfish in order to live it up in one's old age, it is also foolish to "eat, drink and be merry, for tomorrow we die"—when that death may not arrive until fifty years hence. Prudence is a virtue, even if materialism is not. Living one's life before God does not imply living one's life foolishly—quite the opposite.

Jesus applies a strong identifier to the central figure in the parable, calling him a "fool." This word has a background of which Jesus would have been aware.

As Arland Hultgren points out in his commentary on the parables, the word fool is employed in the wisdom literature in the Bible (in, for example, Psalm 14:1: "The fool hath said in his heart, There is no God") to identify those who, unlike the *anawim* (the poor), fail to acknowledge their ultimate dependence upon God. The *anawim*, who depend not in their military power or economic prosperity but on God, may be contrasted with the fool of this parable, who trusted only in himself.[6]

Jesus offers a warning about founding one's sense of security on material things alone, an ultimately futile (foolish) exercise—indeed, an idolatrous one as well.

It is important in this regard not to think that the lesson of this parable is that "all the rich are fools," and not to be tempted to read motives and intentions into the rich fool that simply are not present in the parable. As Hultgren points out, the rich fool is not an exploiter: there is no indication in the text that he is holding back his produce to wait until prices rise. Nor is there evidence that he is unconcerned for others, or withholding generosity.[7] None of this is to be found in the text.

This parable has a contemporary resonance, as it reflects the anxiety that people approaching retirement and old age naturally have about their security, especially at a time in history when people are living longer and more healthily than ever before in human history. We see this worry displayed in TV, radio, online, and print advertisements almost every day: Will I have sufficient resources for a secure retirement and not be a burden on my loved ones or society?

Is this what Jesus is condemning in this parable? I think not. Jesus' words do not constitute a condemnation of unjust manipulation, a lack of generosity, or a concern for a sufficient retirement. Rather, they condemn the fool's materialism and his idolatry in seeing material reality as the source and ultimate guarantee of his security.

The real problem with the rich fool is less that he is rich and more that he was a fool. It is not so much that he was financially wealthy, but that he was spiritually impoverished. It should be obvious that this man's problem was not that he planned for his future but that his vision of what that future would entail was too narrow. His exclusive attachment to the material was the object of reproach. How strange that a man with a broad vision to be able to see and plan for his material well-being was so narrow as to confuse *having* with *being*.

Do successful business executives have an excessive attachment to material goods, which they store up to possess for themselves? It certainly happens. But certain realities of the economic structure that entrepreneurs are acting in actually weaken this tendency. Had our fool understood these, perhaps he would not have been so foolish.

Most businesspeople are competent enough to know that they need to invest a significant percentage of their profits in their business. Kyle Taylor argues in *Entrepreneur* magazine that 50 percent of profits should be reinvested, and Colbey Pfund says in *Forbes*, "Conventional wisdom places the number at around 30 percent of profits—with some people suggesting as high as 50 percent. The actual amount varies but the secret is to reinvest based on an actual strategy as opposed to a set amount/percentage."[8]

The reality of enterprise is that business people are often faced with a choice between their immediate personal desires and the growth of their businesses. If their businesses are to succeed, they must often choose to delay gratification.

The structures of a market economy reward people who act beyond their own immediate desires to look to the needs of others: both the needs of their employers and the needs of the consumers of their products. A businessman who stockpiles his earnings rather than reinvesting a significant portion of them is not going to thrive. Good commercial judgment consists in the ability to anticipate public demand and sacrifice one's own personal immediate profit so that others can access goods and services.

It is not the central concern of this parable—being rich toward God is—but too many preachers simply overlook the potential to reinforce their message with lessons from economic activities in the free market.

This parable also underscores a central (and rather humbling) fact that every investor understands: the future is always uncertain, people don't know what they don't know, and this is why making profits is so difficult. There are no guarantees. There is no enterprise without risk. The past is not a reliable indicator of future performance. Uncertainty about the future is something with which we must all contend. One way to look at this story is to conclude that the rich man was a fool because he believed that he could be certain. He thought he knew things that he could not know. And he was wrong. In this he lacked humility. Our fate is in God's hands, and so we must strive to avoid the conceit that we know the future—as investors, savers, consumers, and policy makers. Of course, this applies to our interior lives as well. We cannot know when our last day on earth will be. We cannot put off acting morally, living properly, freeing our consciences from the effects of sin, making matters right with our neighbors, and committing ourselves to God. We must learn the habit of doing the best thing in front of us. This is what it means to live one's life before God—and eternity.

Our ideals, virtues, and hearts (those intangibles) matter more than our bank accounts. Whether we are rich or poor, we can still live out our highest ideals, shunning avarice and the litigious behavior it so often prompts. What needs to be stored up are good will, benevolence toward neighbors, magnanimity, and transcendent concerns. There will come a time for each of us when this world will no longer contain us, and we will wish we had acted in that way.

There is an ancient Roman tradition that when Caesar returned from some successful battle, a page would accompany him in his chariot. As all of Rome shouted the victor's praises, the little boy would whisper into Caesar's ear repeatedly: "*Memento mori, sic transit gloria mundi!*"—"Remember your death, all earthly splendor fades." It kind of puts things in perspective, doesn't it?

CHAPTER 6

The Two Debtors

"And, behold, a woman in the city, which was a sinner, when she knew that Jesus sat at meat in the Pharisee's house, brought an alabaster box of ointment, and stood at his feet behind him weeping, and began to wash his feet with tears, and did wipe them with the hairs of her head, and kissed his feet, and anointed them with the ointment. Now when the Pharisee which had bidden him saw it, he spake within himself, saying, This man, if he were a prophet, would have known who and what manner of woman this is that toucheth him: for she is a sinner. And Jesus answering said unto him, Simon, I have somewhat to say unto thee. And he saith, Master, say on. There was a certain creditor which had two debtors: the one owed five hundred pence, and the other fifty. And when they had nothing to pay, he frankly forgave them both. Tell me therefore, which of them will love him most? Simon answered and said, I suppose that he, to whom he forgave most. And he said unto him, Thou hast rightly judged. And he turned to the woman, and said unto Simon, Seest thou this woman? I entered into thine house, thou gavest me no water for my feet: but she hath washed my feet

with tears, and wiped them with the hairs of her head.
Thou gavest me no kiss: but this woman since the time I
came in hath not ceased to kiss my feet. My head with oil
thou didst not anoint: but this woman hath anointed my
feet with ointment. Wherefore I say unto thee, Her sins,
which are many, are forgiven; for she loved much: but to
whom little is forgiven, the same loveth little. And he said
unto her, Thy sins are forgiven. And they that sat at meat
with him began to say within themselves, Who is this that
forgiveth sins also? And he said to the woman, Thy faith
hath saved thee; go in peace." (Luke 7:37–50)

L et's cut to the chase. What we have in the Parable of the Two
Debtors is an image of God as a banker, or a money lender.
But he is a money lender whose primary concern is not with
money, but with the well-being of vulnerable people.

The actual parable portion of this story is surprisingly brief, set
in the context of the interaction of Jesus with his disciples. Nevertheless, the Parable of the Two Debtors is pregnant with insight about
sin and forgiveness, and employs the notion of "debt" in relation to
forgiveness, which, when you think about it, is also an important
subject in our day. It is intriguing and timely how this parable raises
the extent to which our values, so often seen in economic terms,
reveal who we really are.

The figure of the 'sinful' woman in this passage has become the
occasion of much confusion: there has been a great deal of speculation regarding her identity over the centuries of Christian reflection
and debate. Some have thought her to be the woman caught in the
adulterous act described in John 8:1–11; others see her as Mary of
Magdala, the evidently wealthy woman from whom seven devils had

been exorcized; and some have identified her with Mary, the sister of Martha and Lazarus of Bethany. Reading the portrayals of Jesus' relationship to women throughout the Gospels sheds light on how these confusions could have arisen. (See, for example, Matthew 26:6–13, Mark 14:3–9, and John 12:1–8.)

Pharisaical law would have considered the woman's touch in the events under consideration in the text a form of defilement of Jesus. Yet Jesus takes a strikingly more generous and forgiving view of this woman, regarding her actions as an expression of love, sorrow, and virtue. To his mind, she is not to be judged based on her past but based on her present actions and aspirations. The degree of her sinfulness, the intensity of her sinful behavior in the past, and her poor reputation, however deserved, are not, for Jesus, determinative of her inherent dignity as a person. She is so obviously seeking redemption. The lavishness in her tender treatment of Jesus reveals something about her values; it is concomitant with (and perhaps proportional to) her awareness of her reputation and her failings.

The action takes place at a banquet. It was the custom to invite travelers, especially preachers at local synagogues, to attend such dinners.[1] The very idea of a woman of doubtful reputation attending such a gathering was countercultural, and this woman adds to the drama by her actions, which were considered unlawful—unfurling her hair in front of men and touching Jesus. And then Jesus demonstrates a depth of charity and pardon for her in public: he alters her moral status by forgiving her past sins and turns what others see as a sensually provocative act into a virtue. Jesus sees her driving motivation as a deep love, illustrative of a change in her heart. She places a higher value on her love for Jesus than the extravagant cost of the perfume. Seeing her motive prompts Jesus' benevolent response.

At this juncture the metaphor of debt arises: To illustrate why he forgave rather than condemned her, Jesus relates the economic image

The Unmerciful Servant, print, after John Everett Millais, engraved and printed by the Dalziel Brothers. *Metropolitan Museum of Art*

of two debtors. One owed perhaps fifty days' wages, and the other owed five hundred days' wages, and both were forgiven by the creditor. Jesus asks his cynical hosts an almost rhetorical question: Which of these debtors has benefited the most from this generosity? Anyone who can add can see that it is the one who had the most debt. This much is rather obvious, and Simon answers Jesus' question correctly. The very fact that the correct answer is so obvious illustrates just how controversial Jesus' actions were. Rather than tell a complex story with a counterintuitive or unclear point, Jesus tells a very straightforward story where the lesson is difficult to miss. Yet consider what it reveals about the character and identity of the creditor.

The parable, like numerous others, serves to illustrate Christianity's perspective on sin and forgiveness. A distinctive feature of Christianity is its insistence upon the universality of the offer of forgiveness, not conscribed to a tribe or a clan, but to all. No matter how egregious the sin or offense, the universal offer of redemption is always made—indeed, even available at the last moment (Luke 23:33–43). The greater the debt, the more generous and praiseworthy is the act of debt forgiveness. This reveals the character of a loving God.

In Christianity, the debt and its forgiveness are not transactional, because they are not a speculative exercise. Rather, the forgiveness reveals the character of God. We can gain insight by employing a comparison to the economic world, where debt is necessarily predicated on transactions based on assurances that reduce the risk involved in making the loan in the first place. Jesus draws heavily from the world of economics to make his points concerning gratitude and proportionality, if for no other purpose than to show the immensity of God's generosity and to incite that quality in us. In the act of redemption, God cancels out the punishment that human beings justly merit for their sins. The reciprocal gratitude for this grace (unmerited favor) naturally increases in proportion to our wrongdoing. The more forgiveness that is required, the more we appreciate its miracle, and the more humility we experience in the face of such mercy. Our love is increased by our awareness of the *cost* of the mercy.

There is a popular and simplistic prejudice—arising from a mindset that has no reference to the transcendent—against creditors, who are often portrayed as the idle rich inflicting damage on the industrious poor. In the Parable of the Two Debtors this popular prejudice is turned on its head. There is no class warfare of the exploiter versus the exploited here. Nor does this parable suggest that the creditor is not due payment, as a matter of pure justice. In fact, his benevolence is seen precisely in the fact that he is. Those who contracted the debt still owe the debt. Without this premise, the parable has no point; it certainly would not be nearly as moving. What occurs here is a notable act of charity, redolent with beauty, instructiveness, and inspiration.

In today's political culture, our sympathies are usually drawn to those who owe money, to those who are seen as being weighed down with an unfair burden, especially when they are required to pay interest. Legislation of all sorts—whether bankruptcy laws, restrictions on "usury," or inflation that is designed to lighten debtors' loads—favors those who carry debt. In the popular imagination the person or institution that extends credit is never seen as a benefactor, or as someone who makes it possible to acquire resources to provide for life's necessities or to spur economic progress.

From a moral perspective, it is understandable, and laudable, that empathy with the vulnerable pervades the human community, regardless of what causes that vulnerability. This empathy, however, does not grant us the right to distort reality. We see no bias on Jesus' part for or against one party or the other. It is as though the Lord has the admonition of impartiality from Leviticus 19:15 in mind: "thou shalt not respect the person of the poor, nor honor the person of the mighty."

Given the pervasiveness of economic activities in most of human life, it is understandable that people have a propensity or temptation to identify their very selves with their status or class. Perhaps no social philosopher has written more radically and with greater effect on the matter of class identity than Karl Marx.[2] Essentially, Marx saw the identity of a person through the lens of that person's economic and social relationships to others. This led Marx to think in terms of the conflicts that emerge between groups (what he calls "class struggle"). Christianity has a very different anthropology, promoting not conflict or class warfare but harmony and reconciliation through interpersonal encounter. This is what we see happening in this parable—even in the economic assumptions being employed.

In contradistinction to Marx, with the advent of the Industrial Revolution the relationship between the debtor and the creditor came to be seen as simply a matter of mutually beneficial exchange, rather than a fixed hierarchy, with the parties' identities determined by class. In this way, the creditor, in having funds, can make those available to the borrower to provide for immediate needs. With the eventual emergence of investment portfolios, where even people of modest means can participate and themselves become creditors, a more holistic picture appears.

Creditors have to examine the financial records and reputation of those who borrow money in order to ascertain how likely it is that the borrower will fulfill his or her end of the deal. Failing to do so will result in an irresponsible and wasteful use of the creditor's own resources.

Nothing in this parable questions the practices of lending and borrowing. And while charging interest on loans, particularly to the poor, had been condemned in the Hebrew Scriptures, Jesus does not condemn interest—which is only the price that the borrower pays for having money at his disposal sooner rather than later—in this parable.[3] He doesn't approve it either; he does not mention it. The charging of interest would *later* become a great moral controversy that tied up early medieval history. Much of the controversy is caused by the failure to understand that a market rate of interest is a natural economic phenomenon and a normal feature of any economic exchange that requires coordination through time.

Legislation that imposes restrictions on the creditor's ability to collect debts introduces a moral hazard that hobbles people's ability to engage in commerce. The debtor becomes less cautious about borrowing and more reckless in his financial dealings. The impact extends to all the creditor's clients. The creditor, in turn, becomes less likely to make loans, or perhaps feels the need to charge a higher rate of interest to insure against the higher risk incurred. This produces a deleterious overall effect in any society, and it is precisely *at this point* that legitimate concerns over "usurious" rates of interest arise. Note, however, that this dynamic is put in motion not by the free functioning of markets. On the contrary, it is the well-intentioned yet restrictive legislation that sets the cycle in motion.

It is only natural that bankruptcy laws, for example, which permit the borrowers to write off loans and not pay their debts have, *inter alia,* made it easier and more likely for people to run up large debts. Common sense tells us that when people's assets are not really at stake, they are more likely to carry debt than when they actually have to pay their debts. The tendency to incentivize people to live beyond their means and accumulate debt is the result of a civic culture that in effect subsidizes it by a vast panoply of legislation enacted allegedly on behalf of those in debt.[4]

The economic facts of this parable are that the two debtors had both made poor decisions, as apparently the creditor had as well. Objectively speaking, the contract had been broken. The borrowers quite possibly couldn't pay the debt even if they wanted to. One borrower was in far worse shape than the other, but they were both in need of help. The creditor knew that he was not going to get paid, and so he ceased to think of his deal as a commercial transaction. This is where the dimension of mercy comes in.

This dynamic is at work in situations that don't involve borrowing money: Let us say that someone calls you to perform some service in exchange for a fee. Perhaps you are an accountant, and you are called to straighten out someone's books. Or perhaps you are an artist and have painted a piece for someone's home. Or let us say that you are a plumber who was contracted to unplug a pipe. These are all business deals, not money-lending situations. But what if it turns out that the person for whom you did the work suddenly admits that he has no money to pay you?

You justifiably may be annoyed. You may take steps to make sure that this will not happen again. You may consider legal action, which is certainly your right. But then, too, something may arise that tugs at your heart. Perhaps it is the unfortunate conditions that led to the breach of contract. Perhaps it is sincerity and transparency on the part of the debtor. Perhaps awareness of some factor beyond the debtor's control broadens your perspective and invites your empathy. Intentions can affect your attitude: Was the debtor deceptive and cunning and intending to cheat at the outset, or did some devastating circumstance intervene? Your response may also depend on your perception of the other person's contrition. It is not inconceivable that you may recall mistakes you yourself have made. You may remember a time when some things beyond your control arose in your own life, making you unable to meet your commitments, or some moment when you found you had just made a bad decision. None of this absolved you of your commitments. But it may have borne on your honesty, the earnestness of your regret, and your willingness to make amends to the extent possible.

What is so often forgotten about the relationship between borrower and lender is that there is a reciprocity between them. The lender has provided a service, and anticipates payment. The borrower has resources he or she would not have otherwise had. (The nature of the economic exchange is the same whether or not money is involved.) In Jesus' parable, it is the lender, not the borrower, who is in a position to make the decision to pursue a legal remedy to the dispute, or alternatively, as seen here, to offer an act of charity. The charitable act itself is made possible by the legitimacy of the debt. This reality of the debt is never challenged by the parable but rather assumed as part of the story. In contemporary thinking, there is a tendency to assume that others outside this freely contracted relationship should be empowered to make these decisions. We often entrust this power to the state, which relieves borrowers of their burden by means of legislation or some other intervention. Whatever the result, it is critical for moral clarity not to confuse government regulation with charity. Legal and regulatory interventions are forms of compulsion from outside the relationship, directed against those who extend credit—essentially, legally exempting customers from paying their bills for groceries, shoes, plumbing services, and the like. Imagine the overall impact this would have on a society that adopted such policies on a wholesale basis.

In our parable, those whose debts are forgiven experience a sense of gratitude toward the lender. In stark contrast to those who agitate for and benefit from government-mandate debt relief, the beneficiaries of the lenders' charity in the parable feel love, not resentment. This is as it should be. We can deepen our appreciation of the moral lesson of this parable by understanding the nature of the commercial contract in question. Creditor-borrower relations are not inevitably a matter of exploitation, and if we see them as such, we will miss the whole point of the story.

If the point is not yet clear, consider how the scenario changes when the debt that is contracted is political. In this scenario, governments borrow from private banks as a means of expanding their spending capacity without having first raised the revenue (in taxes). The debts are paid with future tax receipts. This is why government debt needs to be undertaken with serious and grave consideration, and why it is widely considered so egregious: it involves people in an obligation they never undertook. That is, people who were not party to the debt become obligated to pay it nonetheless. Because this is not a market exchange, when banks call in these loans, the state can only pay them by intensifying its control over the property and lives of its citizens.

It is this reality that gives rise to some moral ambivalence about the problem of Third World debt. It is insufficient to simply say that it must be paid. Paid by whom? At what long-term cost to the population? We can sympathize with those who say it is too large a burden for them to bear. We can also feel sympathy for the banks who extended these loans to the governments in the first place, even as we remember that they can only be paid through confiscating money from people who are far poorer than the bankers.

That doesn't mean that the loans ought to be repudiated, but it does alter our moral assessment somewhat, requiring us to grant that those who say that government debt is unjust have a strong point. The ultimate answer is that governments ought not to borrow excessively, certainly not without the consent of the governed. Like the rest of us, they should not live beyond their means. And that banks also need to keep in mind the moral and economic costs of calling in huge loans in countries where the people are too poor to pay—and of making such loans in the first place.

At the core of this parable is the lesson that charity is a praiseworthy impulse pointing us to a dimension of life that is equally as real as the economic: the debt of love. Here, we encounter persons, not institutions, who were moved to act on behalf of other persons. This is also a reminder that to automatically criticize those who extend loans to those in need is a superficial and uninformed reaction. Such lenders, like all entrepreneurs, assume risks that make advances in living standards for all possible.

Does this parable mean that all pecuniary debts should be forgiven? Whatever one might want to argue in that regard, the fact is that this would be a very different parable if that were its moral. No, it does not mean that. What it does show is that giving people a second chance is morally meritorious. Justice without charity too easily descends into cruelty. On the level of mercy, we can see that the forgiveness of sins is a worthy act of charity, the value of which is increased if the beneficiary shows contrition rather than justifying the sin committed.

Jesus enabled his host Simon (and us) to see the sinful woman as he himself saw her: a person of dignity in need of love and redemption. We are all flawed. In one way or another, we can all be said to be in debt even if only to our parents, who brought us into the world and who first taught us to think and to speak. We are all sinners as well. That is the fundamental lesson of the parable as it applies to our lives.[5] Law and justice have their logic, but charity and true benevolence are what form a distinctly human and decent community. How interesting that Jesus should use an example from the world of finance to illustrate a point so fundamental to Christianity itself. The economic lessons here illustrate that there need be no inconsistency between justice and charity; in fact, they can mutually inform and reinforce one another.

CHAPTER 7

The Talents

"For the kingdom of heaven is as a man travelling into a far country, who called his own servants, and delivered unto them his goods. And unto one he gave five talents, to another two, and to another one; to every man according to his several ability; and straightway took his journey. Then he that had received the five talents went and traded with the same, and made them other five talents. And likewise he that had received two, he also gained other two. But he that had received one went and digged in the earth, and hid his lord's money. After a long time the lord of those servants cometh, and reckoneth with them. And so he that had received five talents came and brought other five talents, saying, Lord, thou deliveredst unto me five talents: behold, I have gained beside them five talents more. His lord said unto him, Well done, thou good and faithful servant: thou hast been faithful over a few things, I will make thee ruler over many things: enter thou into the joy of thy lord. He also that had received two talents came and said, Lord, thou deliveredst unto me two talents: behold, I have gained two other talents beside them. His lord said unto him, Well done, good and faithful servant; thou hast been faithful over a few things, I will make thee ruler over many things: enter thou into the joy of thy lord. Then he which had received the one talent came and said, Lord, I knew thee that thou art an hard man, reaping where thou hast not sown, and gathering where thou hast not strawed. And I was afraid, and went and hid thy talent in the earth: lo, there thou hast that is thine. His lord answered and said unto him, Thou wicked and slothful servant, thou knewest that I reap where I sowed not, and gather where I have not strawed. Thou oughtest therefore to have put my money to the exchangers, and then at my coming I should have received mine own with usury. Take therefore the talent from him, and give it unto him which hath ten talents. For unto every one that hath shall be given, and he shall have abundance: but from him that hath not shall be taken away even that which he hath. And cast ye the unprofitable servant into outer darkness: there shall be weeping and gnashing of teeth." (Matthew 15: 14–30. See also Luke 19:12–27)

The Parable of the Talents may be the most famous of the parables (its only competitor being, perhaps, the Prodigal Son). It is certainly the one that I am most often requested to comment on, given my work in the field of business and economics.

This well-known parable in Matthew's Gospel has a parallel account in Luke 19:12–27, where one finds a number of distinctive and diverse features worth noting, but as the Matthean account is more elaborate, it is more helpful for the limited purpose of this study, as we examine economic presuppositions at play in the parables and probe what thoughts they may prompt in the economic realm.

While the details differ between Matthew and Luke—for example the "man" in Matthew is a "nobleman" in Luke, where a total of eight talents are unequally divided among three servants, as opposed to the ten monetary units equally distributed among ten servants, and so forth—broad similarities remain.

The parable of the talents shares a motif familiar from some of Jesus' other stories, about kings or rulers who go off for periods leaving their wealth to the care and inventiveness to their servants, with varying results (see for example: Mark 13:34–37 and Luke 12:35–38; Matthew 24:45–51, and Luke 12:42–46: and Luke 19:12–27, Matthew 21:33–46, and Luke 20:9–19).

As with all Jesus' parables, we have here many layers of meaning, all of which really come down to lessons on the question of how we are to use what God entrusts to us. On the temporal plane this is a story about capital, investment, entrepreneurship, and the proper use of scarce economic resources, as well as about the risk involved in their employment. The modern mind will raise questions here about equality, but Jesus' world assumed differences. In any case, the parable, like the whole of Christianity, is about the challenge of the unifying power of love. The deployment of this model of business as a simile for the Kingdom of God stands as a direct rebuke to anyone who sees an intrinsic contradiction between business success and the Christian life—even if that is not the point of the parable.

The master in this parable makes his three servants caretakers of his property during his absence. His attention to detail and his meticulousness causes one to suspect that this is not some arbitrary investment but one that he has carefully assessed, concluding that the particular natural abilities of each servant make each one worthy of the trust he is placing in him. He entrusts five talents to one servant, two

The Parable of the Talents by Rembrandt. *The Louvre*

to another, and one to the third, a total of eight talents in all—to each, as we say, "according to his ability"—a phrase critical to understanding the depth of the parable, to my mind.[1] He then leaves the scene for a time. As the servants take on the responsibilities entrusted to them and enter a world open to enterprise and use of their intellects, risk, and investment, their faithfulness comes into focus. The servant who received five talents goes into business and develops his holdings. The servant who received two talents doubles his as well. But the servant who received one talent hides the master's property in a hole in the ground, and it is instructive to discover why. Hiding valuables in the ground was evidently one mode of attempting to preserve one's belongings in ancient Israel, if we are to believe Josephus.[2]

The master returns to settle his accounts, and the servants proceed to give account of their dealings. The first two receive high praise for doubling their investment.

The climax of the drama, of course, occurs when we come to the servant who had been entrusted one talent and who admits he made nothing. His admission almost sounds like a defense, as he points out that the original property was at least kept safe. This servant's explanation gives the impression, that in his mind, not having lost what was entrusted to him fulfilled his commission. The master's response is swift and harsh: he orders that the talent be taken away from the lazy servant and given to the one with the ten talents. He further commands, "And cast ye the unprofitable servant into outer darkness: there shall be weeping and gnashing of teeth" (verse 28).

Our initial reaction to this parable may be to quickly turn to its meaning in the order of salvation: The master who has gone on the journey clearly represents Jesus himself, and the judgment is on our wholehearted fidelity.[3] An eternal reward is granted to those who have been fruitful and faithful stewards of the gifts received. Our work for Christ is expected to be robust, enthusiastic, fearless, and total, aimed at the highest possible result from that with which we have been entrusted. To simply hide this gift is to not employ it; that is obviously not what the gift was given for.

But if we reflect on the plain meaning of the story in an economic sense some additional lessons will emerge as well. Ownership and investment are regular features of life. They are dynamic. If we are contemptuous of the master's intent, or if we prove to be servants unwilling to demonstrate our faithfulness by bringing forth great potential from the master's gifts at one level, how can we prove worthy at a higher level? As the master himself says, "Well done, good and faithful servant; thou hast been faithful over a few things, I will

The Worthless Servant Cast into the Outer Darkness by Léonard Gaultier. *National Gallery of Art*

make thee ruler over many things." This principle applies not just within the realm of economics; it also clarifies the relationship between the material and spiritual realms, both of which must be kept in mind to fully comprehend the lesson in its entirety.

Let's begin with the word "talent" employed here. The English word, which is derived from this parable and came into its current usage in about the fifteenth century, means a capacity or an aptitude.[4]

Consider the size of the sum that Jesus says was entrusted to the care of these servants. In Jesus' time, a Greco-Roman talent was equal to six thousand denarii. A single denarius was the average pay for one day's labor.[5] In other words, this man was given an astounding opportunity to work with an investment equivalent to six thousand days of work.

Calculating on the basis of the current U.S. federal minimum wage of $7.25—which is the very bottom of the pay scale, even for the least challenging jobs—yields a daily wage of $58, making a talent worth at least $348,000. And the master entrusted all three servants with a sum worth at least that much—and the one he gave the five talents to, with an amount equivalent to at least $1.74 million.

In a broader understanding of this parable, the talents are seen as referring to all of the various gifts—natural, spiritual, and material—that God has given us for our use. That would include our natural abilities and resources—our health, education—as well as our possessions, money, and opportunities. It would also cover our personalities, our sense of thrift, our openness to new information (that is, our humility), our wit, and our level of risk-tolerance, among the various aptitudes that are unique to us as individuals. It would include all the traits we possess by virtue of having been created in the image of God, and also all our individual personality traits, small and large, which we take for granted or don't even notice. It might even include our network of contacts, whether we have personally developed or simply inherited them. The list could go on and on. The point is that there is so much in our lives that we benefit from, and that we have received much of it from others or just circumstance—we cannot claim it as our merit alone. It may be that we have had some control of what we have received and perhaps developed or expanded our capacities. But so often they come to us by the fortuitousness of our genetics or geography or by the gifts of others.

Our obligation in the face of such gifts is to recognize them precisely as such. They come with a responsibility to employ them in ways that honor the giver, whether or not the giver is known—and in any case, in ways that serve some higher end or moral *telos*. This is true at both the spiritual and material level. One lesson from the Parable of the Talents is that creativity can be a response of faithfulness and gratitude, and that it is not immoral to profit from our resources. Keep in mind that the alternative to profit is loss—even if it is only a loss of opportunities. Surely a loss, whether of opportunity or of wealth—particularly when it is due to a lack of initiative—does not constitute good stewardship.

This parable presupposes an understanding of the proper stewardship of money. In rabbinical law, burying was regarded as the best security against theft. If a person entrusted with money buried it as soon as he had it in his possession, he would be free from liability if anything should happen to it. The opposite was true for money that was only tied in a cloth. In the latter case, the person was responsible for covering any loss incurred as a result of the inadequate care of the deposit.[6]

Yet this story turns this understanding on its head. If the master wanted the talents buried, he hardly needed to give them to anyone. And he evidently understood that breaking even would actually be a loss—because wealth has potential. That is part of its responsibility. Economically understood, time is money (or interest).

Another lesson of this parable relates to our use of the capacities and resources God entrusts to us—our response to his gift. And this is hardly the first time we see this theme in the Bible. In the book of Genesis, God entrusts to Adam the Earth upon which to apply human labor for the sustenance of the human family—a situation parallel to this parable. Essentially the same thing is seen in the Parable of the Talents, where the master expects his servants to exercise their creativity. Rather than passively hiding what has been given, the servants are expected to invest the money, that is, to be creative with it, applying their minds and labor. The master is angered by the timidity—and the mischaracterization of the master himself—by the servant who had received the one talent and produced nothing with it. Let's take a closer look at this servant.

The lazy servant's characterization of his master is quite revealing. The first thing worth noting is that the fear of his master—on which he will ultimately blame his failure to invest his talent—is not apparent from the outset, when the master initially entrusts his wealth into his care. At that point it would seem that his attitude should be one of appreciation or even pride for being selected for this task. There is no evidence that he sees his master as anything but a generous benefactor with confidence in his servant.

It is only once the servant betrays that trust that he turns on his master. That is, it is when he is called to give an account of his actions that he offers a pejorative assessment—and an inaccurate one as well: "I knew thee that thou art an hard man, reaping where thou hast not sown, and gathering where thou hast not strawed. And I was afraid...." Evidently, the assumption here is that whatever the master owns he has obtained unjustly—not by productive creativity but through some unnamed form of exploitation.

This newly antagonistic attitude, rife with envy and defensiveness, has a good deal in common with our culture's view of our free and prosperous economy. Many of our contemporaries point accusing fingers at the most productive and liberal economic experiment in human history, condemning it for extracting, rather than creating, wealth; accusing it, in effect, of reaping where it has not sown—all the while enjoying the benefits of that bountiful harvest.[7]

Another instructive point in the Parable of the Talents has to do with security. Throughout human history, people have repeatedly attempted to achieve perfect security, just as the failed servant did in this parable. Such efforts have ranged from the Greco-Roman welfare states to nationalist movements of various types and full-scale Soviet totalitarianism down to the Luddite communes of the 1960s. These efforts have not infrequently been embraced by Christians as morally superior solutions for the insecurity that plagues human existence.

Yet in the Parable of the Talents, it is the virtue of courage in the face of an unknown future that is rewarded—in the first two servants, who both doubled the large amounts they were entrusted with by risking them. The first traded the five talents and in doing so acquired five more. It would have been far more secure for this servant to have invested the money in the bank and received interest. But his confidence and accurate knowledge of his master allowed him to keep what had been entrusted to him as well as what he earned, and thus to discover a deeper relationship of joy with his master.

The first servant confronted uncertainty, a persistent and undeniable feature of the world, in an enterprising way. Uncertainty about our future remains an inevitable feature of human circumstances that must be faced with the virtue of courage, determination, and faith. This, perhaps even more than their entrepreneurial activity, is the real virtue of the first two servants. The fear of the unknown so often immobilizes people. People inevitably fail, but it is true to say that there really is no failure worse than never trying at all. For the believer, the cardinal sin of sloth is simply not an option. It is the virtues of faith, hope, and confidence in the face of great odds and obstacles—not greed—that characterize the entrepreneur. Long before he knows whether there will be a return on his investments or ideas, he risks his time and property. In many cases he is willing to risk his whole future and that of his family, yet he sees the risk as commensurate with the potential reward. Imagine what it must be like to pay out wages long before you have a clear idea whether you have accurately predicted that your business will eventually be profitable. People are willing to take such risks because they look to the future with courage and a sense of opportunity. They are attentive and on the alert for new discoveries, innovations, and different ways of doing things. They truly do think outside the box, to the benefit of us all. In the act of creating new enterprises, such people open up alternatives from which workers can choose in order to earn wages, develop skills, and supply needed products and services for human betterment. This is the true meaning of "speculation".

Why, then, are entrepreneurs (like the two servants in this parable) so often castigated as morally inferior exploiters, as selfish and motivated by greed? Of course some investors are so motivated, as are some people in every profession, including in religious institutions. And yet many religious leaders speak and act as if the businessman's use of his natural talents and resources to turn a profit is intrinsically immoral, and as if such profitable activity can only be redeemed to the extent that the profit is somehow redistributed. The Parable of the Talents should disabuse us of this notion.

The lazy servant could have avoided his dismal fate, either simply by declining the master's offer or by emulating instead of castigating his master and being more entrepreneurial. It is intriguing to speculate how the events in this parable might have played out had the servant made an effort to trade with his master's money and come back with less than a talent. It is hard to imagine, given the moral atmosphere of the parable as a whole, that he would have been treated so harshly, for at the very least he would have labored on behalf of his master. A whole new lesson might have emerged that would reassure businesspeople who, having made a good faith effort in their enterprise, nonetheless failed at it, that they ought not to see *themselves* as failures on account of the vagaries of the market. After all, not all failure is moral failure. But instead of trying and failing (or succeeding), he allowed his fear and distrust of the master, based both on envy and illusion, to immobilize him. He never understood his master.

Religious institutions, along with all those whose task it is to form the moral consensus, should recognize entrepreneurship for what it is—a vocation, a calling in need of formation, maturation, and clarity of mission. The ability to succeed in business, stock trading, or investment banking is a talent. Like other gifts, it can be misdi- rected, and it should not be squandered but rather honed and used to its fullest potential for the glory of God. Critics too easily lump financial speculation with greed, yet the fundamental nature of the entrepreneurial vocation is to speculate (from the Latin, *specere:* "to look out"), to focus on the needs of customers—in other words, to be other-directed. To succeed, the entrepreneur must serve others. Indeed, the profits attained in a free economy are an indication of just that: meeting others' needs. If the businessman does not serve others, by those others' own evaluation, he will not be a successful entrepreneur.

Greed is a spiritual hazard, indeed a vice that threatens us all regardless of our wealth or vocation. It is an excessive, inordinate, or insatiable desire for material (and sometimes not just material) gain and satisfaction. When such excessive desire is deep within a person's being, it outweighs all other priorities, moral and spiritual. This parable does not portray profit as unjust—if for no other reason than that the first servant received more than the second and third. The mere making of a profit by the use of one's entrepreneurial talent is not thereby an inordinate desire. It is the proper employment of the talent.

Religious leaders are often heard condemning profit-making. Instead they seem to favor various types of social leveling and the redistribution of income out of concern for "equality." They promote "universal health care," greater social welfare spending, and higher taxes on the rich—all in the name of Christian ethics. The goal of such constructs is human well-being through equality, as if the inequalities that exist among people are somehow inherently unjust and inhumane. But equality is not the message of this parable.

The master entrusted talents to each of his servants according to his particular abilities. This was not really about merit; it was a gift outright, a test of the will and of intensity of desire. Perhaps it was an effort at mentoring. The three servants clearly were not treated "equally"; one received five talents while another received only one. Their abilities also clearly differed. The one who received the least does not receive sympathy from the master for his lack of resourcefulness in comparison to his colleagues. In fact, the identical—that is, equal—commendation to each of the productive servants underscores that the master sought a trusting and creative response to his own trust, rather than simply the most profitable portfolio.

We certainly cannot infer, from this parable at least, that the "equitable" reallocation of resources is a good and moral idea. Here we see that different individuals' having different levels of resources is not inherently unjust. Rampant inequalities are a given—for the simple reason that there are always differences among people. No human being is made exactly like another. We are each distinct, unique, unrepeatable—indeed, precious for being so rare. A moral system is one that recognizes both this splendid diversity and our equal dignity and because of this allows each person to use his or her talents to the fullest and to pursue the particular holiness found in each particular circumstance. Each person possesses a calling that will allow him to employ the faculties, aptitudes, and talents with which he has been endowed. Each is simply called to be faithful, not necessarily successful, as Mother (now Saint) Teresa of Calcutta observed.[8]

There may be a practical application of the lesson in this parable to our own social and economic situation. At present, the pay that workers earn by their labor is taxed to provide support to many who do not work. We often hear that there are "no jobs" for them. How can that be? Where human needs exist, there is always work to be done. A man with two working hands can find work for a dollar an hour—unless he makes a decision not to work. Politicians intending to help the poor have actually accomplished the exact opposite with well-intended but wrong-headed initiatives—high minimum wages that price inexperienced workers out of the job market, for example—put productive work out of the reach of people looking for employment.

Perverse incentives are at play when people are subsidized *not* to work. The pandemic of 2020 is a case in point, when people were actually paid *not* to work, and possibly incentivized not to return to work to some extent by the extension of overly generous subsidies above market wages.[9] Note, this is not about whether we should assist people in need, but rather about the problems created by an *amount* of assistance that is directed in a way that disincentives people to return to work. By the end of 2021, weakened business owners were unable to find workers to employ. If you doubt that, ask the owner of your neighborhood restaurant. God calls all people to use whatever talents they have been given, and under whatever circumstances they find themselves, to benefit the world and their fellow man. Yet in the name of charity and with all kinds of good intentions, our social assistance system so often actually encourages people to let their natural creative and problem-solving skills atrophy, preventing them from even discovering their talents.

It is unimportant whether such policies are publicly or privately funded: any kind of indiscriminate assistance that fails to discern the deepest human need or capacity can inhibit integral human development. When institutions fail to act as neighbors to those in need, and instead act with a materialistic or "bureaucratic mentality," they are encouraging sin.[10]

The Parable of the Talents implies that willing inactivity—or in this case, wasting entrepreneurial talent—has consequences. After all, the lowly servant did not squander his master's money; he just hid it in the ground, something that was entirely permissible in rabbinical law at the time.

Another notable dimension of this story is the severity of the master's reaction to the indolence of the unproductive servant. He calls him "wicked and slothful" and banishes him to the "outer darkness," where there shall be "weeping and gnashing of teeth." Apparently it is not just the servant's sloth that brings such wrath on his head, but his attempt to defend his slothfulness by blaming the master. As we have seen, his excuse for not investing the money placed at his disposal is that his master is hard and exacting—whereas in fact the master placed very generous resources at his disposal. In fact the source of the generosity, the master, is not the root of the servant's problem, which Bible scholar John Meier sums up succinctly: "Out of fear of failure, he has refused to even try to succeed."[11]

Surprisingly enough, there may also be a lesson in macroeconomics here. The master goes on this journey leaving behind a total of eight talents; upon his return the total has become fifteen. This is clearly not a zero-sum game. One person's gain need not be at another's expense. The successful trading of the first servant does not impede the prospects of the third servant. This is true in today's economy as well. In contrast to what is preached from many a pulpit, the success of the prosperous need not come at the expense of the poor.

Had the most successful servant hurt or robbed others in acquiring his profit, it is doubtful that the master would have praised him. A wise use of resources in investment and saving at interest not only benefits the individual, it has a social-economic effect as well. This is President John Kennedy's "rising tide that lifts all boats."

This insightful story, surprising and even alarming in its conclusions, is an allegory of faithfulness to the kingdom and a commentary on the role of personal volition in bringing it about. But the implications extend to the whole of life, and they are applicable to all people. All of us are called to be enterprising, to take prudent risks, and to grow our gifts so as to add to the abundance we and the whole world experience. We are called to be courageous. This is part of what it means to be fully human. The Parable of the Talents illustrates the potential of a free and virtuous economy world-wide, which would extend the wealth of the developed world to those still developing nations.

Not even to try is another way of failing to acknowledge the receipt of the gift in the first place. What is needed is a band of people who are entrepreneurs in moral, spiritual, and material dimensions alike, facing the uncertain future with courage and faith, reforming their own lives as they reform and better the world around them. Then, when the master returns, we will be judged to have been proven faithful.

CHAPTER 8

The King Going to War

"For which of you, intending to build a tower, sitteth not down first, and counteth the cost, whether he have sufficient to finish it? Lest haply, after he hath laid the foundation, and is not able to finish it, all that behold it begin to mock him, saying, This man began to build, and was not able to finish. Or what king, going to make war against another king, sitteth not down first, and consulteth whether he be able with ten thousand to meet him that cometh against him with twenty thousand? Or else, while the other is yet a great way off, he sendeth an ambassage, and desireth conditions of peace. So likewise, whosoever he be of you that forsaketh not all that he hath, he cannot be my disciple." (Luke 14:28–33)

T he Parable of the King Going to War constitutes an admonition on the prudence of calculation—which might also be described as discernment or deliberation. The word "calculation" has acquired a negative connotation in certain contexts, as when we refer to someone as "calculating" in personal relations—implying that such a person is manipulative, that is, lacking in clarity,

Woodcut of the Tower of Babel by an unknown engraver. *British Museum*

transparency, and sincerity in dealing with others. A calculating person has an end game in mind; he is scheming for his own benefit. The calculation being taught in this parable, in contrast, is deliberate consideration of the cost of Christian discipleship. This sort of calculation enables a depth of commitment. The parable provides a most startling answer to the calculation each potential disciple must make: the cost is everything. Everything must be surrendered. Half measures will not suffice. Going halfway and then turning back makes no sense. Better never to have started in the first place. Either we are "all in," as the expression goes, or all out.

This parable is a great example of how Jesus draws us into the story he is telling with something very familiar from everyday life. After all, how many students start college only not to finish? How many homeowners begin repair projects and then abandon them before they are complete, often leaving a greater mess than when they began? Cases of people "throwing good money after bad" abound. Such cases may be educative after the fact, but we have no results to show for them. A task that is defined by its completion is a task that must be taken on from beginning to end. Before we begin a project, then, we have to prepare with a cost estimate and a consideration of whether we really wish to begin it or to begin it at this time, and then we have to have the virtue of perseverance or constancy to see it to the end. The parable, then, is intended as a caution to the disciple: this struggle is going to be hard and long. If we are unwilling to go the distance, we should not begin at all.

The world of economics also exemplifies this principle. The transformation of whole societies from poverty to prosperity via development and production takes place over time; it does not happen instantly. Human beings have the capacity to plan for the future in a way that extends far beyond the capacity in animals. We can think short-term and long-term. We can contemplate ourselves; in fact, we can contemplate our own contemplation. We can trade off short-term gains for a long-term gain that exceeds them. We can choose to contract debts in the present that we anticipate paying off with future revenue streams. These remarkable capacities often account for progress and human betterment.

Our capacity to project and plan allows us to create complex structures of production and construction that extend for years and even generations into the future. Consider the fact that one of the original architects of Saint Peter's Basilica in Rome, Donato Bramante, died about a century before his masterpiece was completed. Market production also requires the ability and stamina to plan ahead, which means anticipating the expected and unexpected. It is the capacity to see the reality of something before it even exists. That is both a responsibility and a burden—as this parable illustrates.

The Parable of the King Going to War connects us to the just war tradition, which requires, among other criteria, a prospect of success: If a nation has no reasonable probability of success in battle, its leaders would be judged to act immorally if they sent their men to their deaths. There must be more than just a chance of winning, there must be a good prospect.

This is only one of a number of strictures requiring a proper discernment or calculation to engage in a just war, but it is particularly praiseworthy.[1]

The postulate under consideration is particularly praiseworthy, for it builds in a bias toward peace. If a country cannot win, it is better to work out terms through diplomacy. Statesmen must not engage in foolhardy imperial adventures. Wise rulers who do not want to waste money and soldiers' lives seek peace. A good calculation is all the more critical when the stakes are high and the consequences resulting from a faulty calculation are likely to be extreme.

The case of the king comes after a more commonplace and perhaps more accessible example of a man who chooses to build a tower in his vineyard. This was probably some form of watchtower and, as such, a kind of luxury good not available to every vineyard owner. The owner decided to build one, but he was of modest income and found himself unable to complete it—wasting resources and becoming an object of ridicule.

Both the Parable of the Tower and the Parable of the King Going to War address the subject of incomplete projects and the need for intelligent planning. Thus they are particularly interesting from the point of view of economics to the extent that they have implications for an issue that vexes the commercial sector: moments when investments go awry, namely recessions and business failures. Plans are made, dreams are dreamt, money is invested, projects are begun, contracts are agreed to, and expansions are contemplated, but then some unanticipated turn of events takes place. The plans are thwarted, money is lost, projects are abandoned, and production is pulled back. Sometimes the result is bankruptcy.

Such business failures can take place on a micro level, when an individual does poorly, or they can occur at a macro level, when an entire economy sinks and businesses fail in the aggregate. In the first case, the business failures may be the result of extravagant spending or a failure to understand the market. This can sometimes occur through outright irresponsibility, but it can also result from bad judgment, incomplete knowledge, or a change in consumer tastes.

For the entrepreneur, the future is always uncertain. It is rare that all the resources are available in advance to complete all projects in process. Most startups fail not for lack of a sound idea but for lack of resources to enable the entrepreneur to push through the first and riskiest stages of his endeavor on to the later revenue stages. There may be insufficient time to gather or produce sufficient resources.

The revenue stream of the business must provide the funds to achieve long-term profitability. If that revenue dries up—something that can happen for any number of reasons—the project must be abandoned.

From the perspective of a pastor, it is worth saying that there is nothing to be ashamed of in any business failure as such. A store that serves the public for a time, making a profit as a result, is a praiseworthy endeavor. But ceasing to be profitable says nothing negative about past real successes—it doesn't cancel them out. It speaks only of the present.

Consider a more puzzling case: an economy-wide recession, when many businesses fail at once. This might be the result of a natural disaster such as a storm or a plague. In modern economies, it is often due to a series of bad choices among an interconnected class of investors, frequently as the result of having been given false signals. Such investors might imagine a bright future with growing consumer demand and a plethora of available capital, but sometimes circumstances change, and neither the demand nor the capital turn out to be as plentiful as they anticipated.

Most businesses invest on credit. That is, they borrow money against a future revenue stream. How much it costs them to borrow money depends on the interest rate, which in turn corresponds to the rate of profit, which in turn is supported by the savings rate. For a successful outcome, entrepreneurs have to keep this three-fold sequence in mind and make the calculations required at each level. The bottom line is that savings are a necessary prerequisite for investment, even when that investment is made on credit. The ability and means to invest must come from somewhere. One cannot loan out or even give away something that is not first produced.

Because the interest rate reflects the savings rate, investors have a pretty good idea of how much in the way of resources will be available in the future to purchase their finished products. They also know how much savings is available to support their credit line. All this information is communicated by the rate of savings and credit. When these signals go awry—as when a central bank manipulates the supply of credit—investors can invest too much too soon and find themselves unable to follow through. The ability to reliably calculate the real costs and risks of investment is enormously obscured and complicated by this kind of interference.

In what economists call "the business cycle," the investment sector becomes overinflated like a bubble. Low interest rates tempt businesses to borrow heavily in hopes of later profits. But the resources to complete the journey turn out to be illusory. Later investments must shrink because the resources are not available to support them. Some examples of this dynamic are the onset of the Great Depression in 1929, the bursting of the dot-com bubble in the late 1990s, and the real estate bust and subsequent financial bust of 2008. It is instructive to see how this phenomenon, recognized by economists only in modern times, makes an appearance in this parable of Jesus.

The parable also underscores a fascinating point about the "time structure" of production. Goods and services do not just appear on the market in a day or week. The production and marketing of even the simplest item requires a tremendous amount of planning. Raw material must be purchased, capital goods acquired, laborers hired, and the marketing of the product plotted and planned. All of this must happen before a single final good can be purchased by a consumer. Whether and to what extent a good or service is profitable is entirely in the hands of consumers, in their capacity as decision makers who buy or refrain from buying based on their own subjective needs. It is the consumers' future decisions that the entrepreneur must calculate at all levels of the trading structure.

It is evident that production in a market economy requires good judgment, long-term planning, calculation, and discernment.

Production requires reliable information and intelligence. It is emphatically not a "dog-eat-dog" contest of consumerism and greed unleashed, as it is so often popularly characterized. It is a complex matrix of exchange that stretches across the whole population, producers and consumers alike, a matrix characterized by cooperation, planning, and judgment. And the time element of production, as this process unfolds, requires as much planning and coordination as any other aspect. It is a delicate balance, carefully calibrated by individual planning which, as we have seen, depends on reliable market signals that are themselves predicated on the information revealed in free exchange and cooperation. When the free market is impeded, and exchanges are based on things other than the free choices of the interlocutors, those signals become distorted, causing discoordination and waste.

Are some people better entrepreneurs than others? Most certainly. The division of labor applies here as it does elsewhere in society. People who behave like the foolish vineyard owner or the king going to war will not last long in the marketplace. Their poor judgment will be costly, imposing unsustainable losses. On the other hand, the market rewards those who make good judgments about the future and plan accordingly. In a sense, people in business must sometimes sell everything they have in order to enact their enterprise. Family businesses in particular are sometimes far more costly than people expect. They take vast amounts of time, and they often require even mortgaging the family home and dipping into retirement savings.

Before a person sets out on any undertaking, he or she should examine not just the initial costs but the long-run costs as well. He will have to look not just at today's expenses and the means he has to pay them, but what it will cost him to reach the end goal. He will have to accept the fact that enterprise requires sacrifice.

All this ought to inspire a deeper respect for successful entrepreneurs than is general in our culture. Entrepreneurs assist in the process of production, raise living standards, fuel economic growth, and economize on resources. Policies that encourage short-sightedness, such as high taxes, immobilizing regulations, and credit expansion are to be avoided because they confuse and obscure market signals necessary to discern the proper conditions for investment.[2] We should do everything we can to allow ourselves to think clearly about the long-term implications of all that we do.

In drawing attention to the necessity of discerning the cost of discipleship, Jesus reminds us to choose well the investments we make. As the magnitude of the potential loss is infinitely greater, so the discernment required for investment is also infinitely greater—because, of course, the consequences are eternal. Christ is asking for the ultimate investment.

Of course, what we might call the "economics of discipleship" must transcend even the kind of sacrifice and surrender that enterprising businesspeople make for the sake of their families, employees, and consumers. When Luke cites Christ as calling for the rich young man to renounce all of his resources, this cannot be a universal requirement of discipleship, given the example that Luke himself provides a mere four chapters later in recounting the example of the wealthy tax collector Zacchaeus, whose declaration that "the half"— not the whole—"of my goods I give to the poor; and if I have taken any thing from any man by false accusation, I restore him fourfold," is approved by Jesus' words: "This day is salvation come to this house, forsomuch as he also is a son of Abraham. For the Son of man is come to seek and to save that which was lost" (Luke 19:1–10).[3] Christ is calling people to something much more radical than merely emptying their bank accounts; he is calling for the surrender of the disciple's heart. Everything else follows from that.

Everything worth having requires sacrifice; our very value for the comforts we enjoy today can yield a great reward commensurate with our investment. To see that requires vision. To achieve that requires courage and commitment.

CHAPTER 9

The House Built on a Rock

"Therefore whosoever heareth these sayings of mine, and doeth them, I will liken him unto a wise man, which built his house upon a rock. And the rain descended, and the floods came, and the winds blew, and beat upon that house; and it fell not: for it was founded upon a rock. And every one that heareth these sayings of mine, and doeth them not, shall be likened unto a foolish man, which built his house upon the sand. And the rain descended, and the floods came, and the winds blew, and beat upon that house; and it fell: and great was the fall of it. And it came to pass, when Jesus had ended these sayings, the people were astonished at his doctrine." (Matthew 7:24–27)

"And why call ye me, Lord, Lord, and do not the things which I say? Whosoever cometh to me, and heareth my sayings, and doeth them, I will shew you to whom he is like. He is like a man which built an house, and digged deep, and laid the foundation on a rock: and when the flood arose, the stream beat vehemently upon that house, and could not shake it: for it was founded upon a rock. But he that heareth, and doeth not, is like a man that without a foundation built an house upon the earth; against which the stream did beat vehemently, and immediately it fell; and the ruin of that house was great." (Luke 6:47–49)

I n this chapter we will consider two versions of what look to be essentially the same parable, albeit including differing details and directed to different audiences. Scripture scholars have researched in great detail the sources from which Matthew and Luke derived their parables and the significance of the differences between the Gospel accounts. For our narrower purpose, however, which is to address any economic assumptions, wisdom, and insight these parables have to offer, those details need not delay us, as admittedly intriguing and important as they are for any fully rounded understanding of the Bible. Here, instead, we will focus on what the accounts in Matthew and Luke have in common.

The moral shared by the versions of the parable in both Matthew and Luke is a lesson in stability in the face of adversity, and a warning to secure the foundation of the edifice one constructs. The theological allusion here is to the Last Judgement, and to whether or not the foundation we have built on will withstand it.[1] Hearing the truth is not enough. We must also be obedient to it; we must put it into practice. That is what secures a person in rough times. A house built on sand might look solid, but when the storms come, the truth is revealed. Only those built on rock will survive.

These images speak directly to our own experience and knowledge. They warn us about the folly of ill-conceived schemes. They conjure up unforgettable pictures of wise and foolish behavior. They cause us to imagine, to think, to reflect, and to apply these lessons to our own lives. Because commerce touches us all in our daily lives, it is precisely from commerce and its context that so many of the lessons of the parables are drawn.

These dramatic parables ask us specifically to consider housing construction. Housing, along with food and clothing, is an essential need for human survival. The need is cross-cultural: the need for shelter from the elements is a problem has been faced in all ages and in all places, and it will be faced in all ages and places to come. This is one reason the story is so relatable. When we move to a new town, we face the problem of housing. There are decisions to be made: To buy or rent? Which part of town to live in? How big? How much to spend? What are the schools like in the area, and how close are they? What is the distance from the residence to the location of our work, and so on? The construction of the house is also critical to its value, which is why we have inspectors and insurance brokers to investigate carefully. Poor construction makes the investment vulnerable.

The story of the wise and foolish builders gives us a little insight into Jesus' own technical knowledge of house building—a skill, interestingly enough, that was not at all different to the carpentry trade. In the ancient world, some people might construct their own homes, but if the homes were substantial, they would no doubt contract out the building of their houses, even if the overall division of labor had not yet fully matured. Today we can live in an adequate, well-built home even if we personally possess few of the skills necessary for construction, such as physical strength and endurance, an understanding of how to make accurate measurements, knowledge of how things fit together to reliably bear weight, and so forth. We can "outsource" these skills today; a personal understanding of them would undoubtedly have been far more necessary in the first century.

The construction of a house is also a matter of time and resources, and tradeoffs have to be faced: Will you build a house with an eye to

He Built on the Sand from *"Blasts" on a Ram's Horn*. Frederick L. Chapman and Co.

speed, putting down roots in ground of less-than-ideal conditions? Or should you hunt for the best possible spot, where the house can be secured against both weather and age?

The metaphor of a solid structure with a firm foundation is, of course, a metaphor for our spiritual and moral lives. By this metaphor Jesus intends the security of knowing him as the "Rock" on which our faith rests (1 Corinthians 10:4). On a less transcendent level, economics comes in to play, which also informs our spirituality. After all, both are choices between expediency and long-term value. Imagine if there were an active market for houses. Buyers would have every incentive to discover how well-built the house truly is. A weak foundation will hurt the long-term value of the house.

This is as true for the owners of the house as it is for the value of the house to the community as a whole. I recall in a Midwestern town there stood a beautiful two-story house built a century ago in a gorgeous Victorian style. It gleamed with its white paint, and its roof was freshly tiled. Its manicured yard was surrounded by a charming fence matching the style of the house. The interior was equally as nice. It was a large place, on an expansive property, lovingly tended. It was a house admired by all.

One day it went on the market—and, as you might expect, at a very high price appropriate for a house of great distinction. It had beauty, age, and grace. Who would be the lucky ones to become the new owners? True, it was priced at the top of the market, but no one doubted for a moment that the owners would get their asking price.

Then came the inspectors, specialists in examining the details of construction. They were working on behalf of the prospective buyers. The report the inspectors gave was grim; it could be boiled down to two words: *cracked foundation*. If you know houses, you know what that means. Even if the next owners could live with the house on a cracked foundation, they would face a skeptical market in the future and never recover their investment in the house. At some point, the house would collapse. There is no point in spending money this way. It would, in effect, be throwing money away. It would be foolish. The value of a solid, reliable foundation is clearly seen here.

What happened to the value of that house? Follow this now: the future value was imputed back to the present, that is, what it could feasibly be sold for at a future date helped determine the present selling price. The selling price became essentially no higher than the value of the land. All this happened in what seemed like an instant. Instead of selling at a high price, the house ended up selling for what the land alone would have cost. It could have been lived in for a time, but the house was torn down and a new one built in its stead. All this took place because of something no one could even see. All the renovations, all the paint, all the careful attention to cosmetics could not overcome that cracked foundation.

This underscores the fact that our parable is not only about how the weather affects building construction. It gets to the heart of what is valuable, both in the here and now of a market economy and also in the transcendent and eternal sense; in the present *and* in the future. No matter how much time one spends making the exterior of a building beautiful, or how much one advertises and promotes it, or how perfect the landscaping, a house that does not have the fundamentals right is one that has no long-term value. Shoddy goods will eventually be found out. Reality is like that.

There are important economic as well as inescapable moral lessons for investors and entrepreneurs here. Going for the quick buck is not even usually the best business decision over the long term. An upfront investment of time and money can result in a greater longer-term benefit. The use of extra resources at the beginning of a project often spares heartache and financial loss later on.

A modern economy can be envisioned as a process of construction or building. Given all the resources we have at our disposal, we still face the decision about how to use them wisely. We do well to emulate the model of the wise builder in this parable, who finds land that comprises a solid foundation on which to build. And this is not only because it is in our self-interest to protect our property, our reputations, and the value created by our labor. There is also a broader and more wide-ranging effect: It is in the interest of the whole society for us to plan wisely. As each of us works prudently, together we will see the value of all resources rise over time. By building on rock and not sand, we contribute to an enduring prosperity.

The transcendent moral and dimension of this parable is clear. Appearances can be deceiving. If we are going to have a solid, reliable future, the solidity of our faith must be at the very foundation of our lives, of all our thoughts, words, and deeds. We must give the foundation attention so as to ensure the future. The informative relationship between the commercial life of this parable and its spiritual import is rich and valuable in showing us how to seamlessly interweave our technical capacities with our transcendent goals.

CHAPTER 10

Lessons in Stewardship

"And the Lord said, Who then is that faithful and wise steward, whom his lord shall make ruler over his household, to give them their portion of meat in due season? Blessed is that servant, whom his lord when he cometh shall find so doing. Of a truth I say unto you, that he will make him ruler over all that he hath. But and if that servant say in his heart, My lord delayeth his coming; and shall begin to beat the menservants and maidens, and to eat and drink, and to be drunken, the lord of that servant will come in a day when he looketh not for him, and at an hour when he is not aware, and will cut him in sunder, and will appoint him his portion with the unbelievers. And that servant, which knew his lord's will, and prepared not himself, neither did according to his will, shall be beaten with many stripes. But he that knew not, and did commit things worthy of stripes, shall be beaten with few stripes. For unto whomsoever much is given, of him shall be much required: and to whom men have committed much, of him they will ask the more." (Luke 12:42–48)

"Who then is a faithful and wise servant, whom his lord hath made ruler over his household, to give them meat in due season? Blessed is that servant, whom his lord when he cometh shall find so doing. Verily I say unto you, that he shall make him ruler over all his goods. But and if that evil servant shall say in his heart, My lord delayeth his coming; and shall begin to smite his fellow servants, and to eat and drink with the drunken; the lord of that servant shall come in a day when he looketh not for him, and in an hour that he is not aware of, And shall cut him asunder, and appoint him his portion with the hypocrites: there shall be weeping and gnashing of teeth." (Matthew 24:45–51)

"And he said also unto his disciples, There was a certain rich man, which had a steward; and the same was accused unto him that he had wasted his goods. And he called him, and said unto him, How is it that I hear this of thee? give an account of thy stewardship; for thou mayest be no longer steward. Then the steward said within himself, What shall I do? for my lord taketh away from me the stewardship: I cannot dig; to beg I am ashamed. I am resolved what to do, that, when I am put out of the stewardship, they may receive me into their houses. So he called every one of his lord's debtors unto him, and said unto the first, How much owest thou unto my lord? And he said, An hundred measures of oil. And he said unto him, Take thy bill, and sit down quickly, and write fifty. Then said he to another, And how much owest thou? And he said, An hundred measures of wheat. And he said unto him, Take thy bill, and write fourscore. And the lord commended the unjust steward, because he had done wisely: for the children of this world are in their generation wiser than the children of light. And I say unto you, Make to yourselves friends of the mammon of unrighteousness; that, when ye fail, they may receive you into everlasting habitations. He that is faithful in that which is least is faithful also in much: and he that is unjust in the least is unjust also in much. If therefore ye have not been faithful in the unrighteous mammon, who will commit to your trust the true riches? And if ye have not been faithful in that which is another man's, who shall give you that which is your own? No servant can serve two masters: for either he will hate the one, and love the other; or else he will hold to the one, and despise the other. Ye cannot serve God and mammon." (Luke 16:1–13)

These three pericopes from Matthew and Luke's gospels provide us with an opportunity to reflect on some varied dimensions of stewardship and entrusted responsibility, from both negative and positive perspectives. The striking similarity of Matthew and Luke's accounts of the Parable of the Faithful Steward permits us to take the two versions of it together. Comparisons between the Parable of the Expectant Steward in Luke, the very similar Parable of the Faithful Servant in Matthew, and the related Parable of the Unjust Steward, also in Luke, and speculations about their employment of common source material intrigue Biblical students and scholars, as they should. But given our more attenuated purpose here, we will take a step back from these details and look at the big picture, so as to ascertain what lessons can be learned or comparisons drawn to the world of finance and economics.[1]

Postilla Guillermi super Epistolas et Evangelia by Urs Graf. *British Museum*

All three parables are stories about fidelity: the master of a household entrusts his possessions to a head servant. The faithful servant fulfills the trust placed in him, while the unfaithful servant takes advantage of the situation and indulges in some egregious actions: gluttony and pride or, in the case of the unjust steward, downright and cunning exploitation of the master's property. In the drunkenness and physical abuse of the other servants, we see two common behaviors of people who imagine that they are unaccountable. They devour wealth and indulge in abusive power relationships over others, as well as manifesting intemperance. All this reveals an even more fundamental vice antithetical to discipleship: unfaithfulness. We especially see this in the interior thought process of the unfaithful steward. Similar interior monologues are seen in other Lukan parables, which we will explore in more detail in due course.

In rich households, it was common for reliable servants ("slaves" in some translations) to be placed in charge of the management of all the household work and accounts in return for which they received a fixed allotment of food and housing. Even in the Greek and Roman tradition, they would not be treated cruelly or beaten wantonly. However, in the case of the unjust servant, his abuses are exposed and in return he is rendered the same treatment he gave to those under him.[2]

The image of the master here is the embodiment of the moral law that holds all things accountable. It is common for people to go about their lives with their immediate attention on the micro-realities confronting them, thinking that it will be a long time before they will be held to account for transgressions; more and more people, it would seem, believe they may never be held to account at all. Reality, however, is a stubborn thing, it will not be ignored. Each one of us will be found out. A moment will come when we must give an account of our faithfulness.

These parables can also be seen as a warning against any form of abusive power that imagines itself to be unaccountable. Corrupting power devours as much wealth as it can—and devours people in the process as well. Certainly this is seen in the long history of coercive power unlimited and unaccountable to any higher authority. Governments in particular, especially given their enormous size, frequently act like the evil servants in these parables, who think themselves to be acting in secret. Their assumption that they are unaccountable cloaks the very sort of abuses recounted in the parables.

Trust, the basis of faithfulness, is the glue of all positive relationships, including commercial life—which is simply an extended network of relationships. Trust holds businesses together and makes possible the relationships between debtors and borrowers, renters and owners, workers and proprietors, benefactors and recipients, management and stockholders. All of these relationships demand a great deal of trust that others will carry out their end of the bargain, be responsible and honest, follow through with their commitments, and behave uprightly.

Whether a landlord is looking for a tenant, a car dealer is considering extending credit, or a business owner is looking for a manager, the first thing desired, in one way or another, is evidence of past behavior, by which to gauge the person's present trustworthiness. We look at credit reports, references, and testimony from others with whom the person has had dealings, because we are seeking a faithful steward.

The "faithful" steward in Matthew and Luke fulfills the trust of his benefactor by taking good care of the property while the owner is away, even when he does not know the date of his return. This steward feels a sense of responsibility whether he is being observed or not. He can be depended upon to take care of what is entrusted to him and to live up to his agreement to abide the master's expectations. This is the kind of person who most often thrives in the long term in every area of life. In the contemporary context, this is the person who is most likely to have a good credit record, who advances in businesses and ascends the corporate ladder. He is the kind of person with whom others want to do business. Of course, this is not universally the case—particularly where some kind of subterfuge, dishonesty, institutional prejudice, or coercion is introduced into the picture.

The question these twin parables raise, with respect to faithfulness, is whether a person would remain a good steward if he sensed the owner would not be overseeing his affairs and was away for an extended period of time; in other words, is he trustworthy even when there is no higher authority to whom he is accountable? Does he see himself accountable to a higher standard or authority?

Would you still pay your debts on time if you knew that failing to do so would not damage your credit rating? Would you trash an apartment you were renting if you knew that the owner had no recourse for recompense or would never know who had destroyed his property? Would you manage a company poorly if the stockholders would never find out or didn't care? Many people drive rental cars or use public toilets with this mentality. We see this when an enforceable right to property is obscured or weakened.

Let's take the case of a company whose shares are traded publicly. The CEO and his staff, including all the vice presidents, are not owners (or, to put it more precisely, their title alone does not itself ensure ownership). Essentially, they are managers, employees, or stewards—not unlike those presented in the parable. The real owners are the stockholders. It is the stockholders who are in charge of determining the structure of management. The problem arises in that this control is a last resort because it is exercised remotely.

A great deal of damage can take place within a company if its managers do not believe that the stockholders are paying close attention, particularly if the managers are not inherently trustworthy. The managers—the CEO and his staff—have what is called a "fiduciary" responsibility to the stockholders. This word has its root in the Latin *fiduciaries, fiducia,* and *fidere,* all of which speak of trust or being "entrusted" with something by someone. The managers are supposed to act out of a "sense of ownership," even without legal ownership. Their role is critical and requires trust, for example during a stock market boom. Stockholders can become reckless and wanton, believing that a higher and higher price confers some sort of legitimacy on a company even when its balance sheet is in terrible shape.

When the bust comes, things change. Stockholders become fiercely combative. They finally examine balance sheets closely. They demand accountability for every dime spent. They are intolerant of recklessness and bad decision making. It is precisely this state of affairs that one senses in the parables' warning of the impeding return of the master or "lord." The date may be uncertain. But as we've seen frequently during economic downturns, corporate scandals emerge as management can no longer hide their defects and find themselves under serious fire.

Corporate managers can behave as "faithful stewards" by putting the company on a firm financial footing, not an illusory one, using resources wisely even when the stockholders are not paying attention, and treating the company's property as though it were their own. Or they can behave like "unfaithful stewards," breaking faith and squandering the resources with which they have been entrusted.

It is not necessary to go to the corporate level to see the truths contained in this parable at work. These principles play out in the corporate world, for sure, but also in shops and groceries, and—as any pastor and parent knows—even in churches, or in homes, particularly when parents leave a teenager in charge. Every role comes with responsibilities. Every worker must ultimately monitor himself or herself. This is especially true in a developed economy, when so many workers sit behind terminals and have innumerable opportunities for doing things other than what they were hired to do, or when, more recently, so many have had to work from home. When we are paid to accomplish certain tasks, when we freely contract to perform those tasks, but instead use the time for other extraneous purposes, much less than for self-aggrandizement, we are acting as unfaithful stewards.

These parables contain strong implications for each of us: workers, management, clergy, families, and everyone else. We are all stewards in one way or another, including within our homes. There are also particular political implications here. Politicians who imagine themselves to be unobserved and unaccountable will become corrupt and authoritarian, engaging in exploitative behavior toward their constituents and their property.

If we look specifically at the dishonest steward of Luke 16, some more complex lessons arise. Once his betrayal is uncovered, he finds himself confronted with the dilemma of how to survive. The truth about a person's character and values is often revealed only in these kinds of existential situations.

It is clear that this imposed transparency does not alter the unjust steward's basic nature. He remains cunning, innovative, and talented. It might well be these same talents that the master initially saw as promising in him, prompting his hiring in the first place, and giving him a high position with a great deal of responsibility.

Let's look at some often-blurred distinctions between a person's abilities and his character, which may make this parable clearer. The complex reality is that efficiency, while a desirable trait in economic terms, when executing a job or trying to make an enterprise successful, is not necessarily a moral good when trying to live an upright life. The flip side is true as well: inefficiency, certainly undesirable in a business setting, is not necessarily a moral failure. All this is to say that an evil person may succeed in his or her business endeavors while a moral and decent person may fail in the same endeavors—and do so without moral culpability.

We see this in productive market economies where people are permitted to cooperate and share their knowledge and talents with one another. Even participants who are immoral, vain, or lacking in decency may succeed in producing high levels of prosperity.

Or the contrary may occur, when deeply pious, kind, generous, and moral participants are caught in centrally planned system—"caught," because the very nature of such systems is coercive—and can never achieve prosperity because of an economic system that makes prosperity impossible.[3] Such people are innocent of the waste and corruption in which they find themselves embedded.

These subtleties and the layers of injustice and immorality within these differing systems, which are too often lost sight of in debates over, and moral condemnation of, markets, can be seen at play in this text.

Many who read the Parable of the Unjust Steward are perplexed by Jesus' commendation of the dishonest steward for doing "wisely"— for his "shrewdness" or "prudence," as some translations have it. What could Jesus possibly mean?

The Greek word translated as shrewd or prudent here is *phronimos*, the same word used in Matthew 10:16, where it is often rendered as "wise," as in "wise as serpents, and harmless as doves." Of course, the image of a serpent in the Bible is most often seen as negative (see Genesis 3:1, 14; Exodus 7:8; Numbers 21:4–9; 2 Kings 18:4; Mark 6:18; Acts 28:3–6, and Revelation 20:2), so in neither Luke nor Matthew would we be warranted in thinking that this is an endorsement of the other qualities of the Devil, as Pablo Gadenz points out.[4]

Rather, the gospel writers evidently see the possibility that someone can be both dishonest yet shrewd or prudent, even *more* shrewd or prudent—"wiser"—than Jesus' own disciples, to whom the Lord is directing this lesson. The master's commendation of the unjust steward for his prudence or shrewdness—for doing "wisely"—is not an endorsement of his dishonesty, but a focus on the talent he possesses, which if employed for a good end would be commendable.

Some commentators attempt to ease this tension by either exonerating the steward (who, they argue, was falsely accused of corruption) or by justifying the expropriation of the master's property, given that the rich master was simply too rich.

Such attempts only serve to diminish the profundity of the challenge Jesus is proposing. First, here is an unappealing, self-centered character who never even professes his innocence, but rather deepens his guilt as he goes about expropriating the master's property one last time, in order to secure his retirement by reducing the evidently extensive debts owed to the master. He thus cheats the master for his own benefit and involves others in his scheme. The whole point of this parable is that the steward *is* dishonest. And it is from within the framework of this very dishonesty that he is planning his future.

The question for the disciple who is outside that framework is: Am I as creative and innovative as the unjust steward is, but for the good?

Prudence is the use of reason to manage affairs. It is a good in itself, but a moral evaluation of what is achieved by its application depends on the end, finality, goal, or *telos* of the action.[5] Jesus seeks to impart to his disciples the importance of diligence, practicality, and talent through the dissonant example of a savvy yet dishonest servant who, from within his own (unjust) character can ensure that he can enjoy the hospitality of his master's debtors. Jesus thereby asks his disciples to draw a lesson from this as how they might store up "treasure in the heavens that faileth not" (Luke 12:33).

The sins of unjust stewards, corporate managers, and public officials are only examples of a larger problem. Everyone faces the temptation to avoid responsibility, accountability, and judgement. Having neither invented nor created ourselves, we find we are only stewards of what we possess and even of what we are, including not only the world but our own bodies. We must care for and cherish all the things entrusted to our care preeminently for the benefit of the supreme good: our souls. Prudence, honesty, and faithfulness are what are required in this life. We need to exercise those virtues habitually, even when we think no one is looking and when no one will find out how we are behaving. This is the definition of what it means to be good steward.

CHAPTER 11

The Good Samaritan

"A certain man went down from Jerusalem to Jericho, and fell among thieves, which stripped him of his raiment, and wounded him, and departed, leaving him half dead. And by chance there came down a certain priest that way: and when he saw him, he passed by on the other side. And likewise a Levite, when he was at the place, came and looked on him, and passed by on the other side. But a certain Samaritan, as he journeyed, came where he was: and when he saw him, he had compassion on him, And went to him, and bound up his wounds, pouring in oil and wine, and set him on his own beast, and brought him to an inn, and took care of him. And on the morrow when he departed, he took out two pence, and gave them to the host, and said unto him, Take care of him; and whatsoever thou spendest more, when I come again, I will repay thee. Which now of these three, thinkest thou, was neighbour unto him that fell among the thieves? And he said, He that shewed mercy on him. Then said Jesus unto him, Go, and do thou likewise." (Luke 10:30–37)

We come to what is undoubtedly one of the most famous—and unusually clear—parables of Jesus: The Good Samaritan. There is hardly a soul in Christendom, or even outside of Christendom, who is unfamiliar with the story. The plain meaning of the parable is a dramatic lesson in solidarity: we are all brothers who share one Creator and merit the recognition of our intrinsic dignity but are also vulnerable and thus at some point will be in need of charity from others—and thus we are, reciprocally, morally bound to grant charity to others. It may be tempting to assume there is no need to probe the context or linger long over the narrative itself. Given that the message of the parable is so clear, diligent exegesis may seem to be unnecessary. But over and above the clear model of conduct we find in the Parable of the Good Samaritan, this compelling story does indeed offer the attentive student a rich reward.

At a time when people were often radically separated by tribe, class, religion, family, and social status, Jesus insisted we should reach beyond such boundaries and love our neighbor as we love ourselves. The very fact that this lesson seems to us so intuitively right is evidence of the sustained impact of Jesus' teaching.

When he was asked, "Who is my neighbor?" Jesus replied that anyone was eligible.

There is a subtle yet crucial correlate to the question being posed to Jesus by his interlocutor (setting aside the issue of that interlocutor's sincerity). He is asking to whom he has a moral obligation: "Who is my neighbor?" But that question also subtly implies another: Who is *not* my neighbor? That is, to whom do I owe nothing?

The limits on our resources, time, and energy are contingencies imposed on us by the finitude of our existence. The limits on our love and compassion are not; one lesson of this parable is that our compassion ought to be boundless.

I imagine that this story, found only in Luke's Gospel, inspires almost anyone who reads it to think that we would behave like the Samaritan in the same circumstances. Certainly, the original audience for this parable was impressed by the Samaritan's compassion and saw that he had done the right thing.

Neither religion, nor class, nor nationality was the determining factor that prompted his actions, but a simple concern for another human being in need, created in the image and likeness of a common Father. Scholars tell us that the man who was beaten would most certainly have been a Jew. Jews had tense relations with Samaritans, even if at times they engaged in commerce with them, Josephus reports.[1] What makes the cultural separation all the more intriguing is that Samaritans and Jews were genetically close, but theologically and liturgically distant. Yet the Samaritan treats the Jew not merely with common civility, but with extraordinary charity. He is willing to extend himself beyond the cultural boundaries and expectations in place at the time.

This long stretch of road from Jerusalem to Jericho has a drop of some 3,500 feet. Traveling along it was so risky that it would not ordinarily have been traversed except for business necessity or some other important reason. There is a suggestion here that the Samaritan knew the region, given his acquaintanceship with the local inn owner; it may have been a common trek for him. The Samaritan is described as having sufficient financial resources to cover the costs for the victim's rehabilitation. Once again, as in the Parable of the Talents, the use of a particular monetary unit suggests that the measure of moral investment is notable. Consider the magnitude of this charity: two denarii or two days wages, with a guarantee for further reimbursement if required. Scholars estimate this would have equaled the victim's need for a one- or two-weeks' recuperation.[2]

The Good Samaritan by William Hogarth. *Royal Academy*

Whether we conceive of the Samaritan as simply a parabolic device to make clear the story's meaning or as an actual person, he remains at the moral center of the drama as most probably a business man as well—two unexpected features for a hero.[3] This helps to clarify the context of the story.

People are often inclined to think of the Samaritan as an archetype for the modern social worker or the personification of a welfare agency (more on this in a moment). But as the parable is constructed, it makes much more sense that the Samaritan was a businessman, thus drawing on a theme that traces to commerce. The source of the wealth that enables the Samaritan to behave charitably was his own enterprise, and it is this ethos of enterprise that serves as the basis and capacity for his charitable impulses. So, whether he is an historical figure or a literary one, the Samaritan anchors the moral sense and charitable center of the story.

This is an especially salient point whenever when we are tempted to somehow juxtapose commerce with charity. This story affords us a way of approaching the parable so as to unify both worlds by seeing how they might reinforce each other; this story show us how they very well may go together. After all, one normative means we have of getting to know others and coming to appreciate their merits and humanity is commercial relationships of mutual benefit. Commerce, one of the most common forms of social engagement, accustoms us to treating others as valuable, and may more readily dispose us to be touched and moved by the suffering of others.

A question to ask ourselves personally is, do we act as the Samaritan did? Do we treat people as we want to be treated ourselves? Are we prepared to prioritize or just be interrupted by the needs of others? In the normal course of the day, it is helpful and enriching to think of our co-workers, bosses, employees, and those in our communities of all classes and backgrounds as people who might themselves be in need or might be called upon to provide care to others. We can prepare for unexpected calamity, such as what befell the victim in the story, by fostering harmonious relations with others. This might even be considered a form of social insurance.

This has particular bearing on the professional workplace. We have all had co-workers who became ill or faced some unforeseen private disaster. We may have been asked to cover for them while they were away or to otherwise make sacrifices on their behalf, even when we weren't compensated for it. In fact, this is not an unusual experience. This is an opportunity to gladly undertake such challenges, not only because morality demands it of us, but due to something we know innately: Each of us has needs, and to be willing to

The Good Samaritan by Rembrandt. *Rijksmuseum*

recognize that in others is called solidarity. We simply never know when others will be asked to do the same on our behalf.

This story could also have application for those who tend towards conflictual relationships with people who are higher up or lower down the chain of management in a particular business firm. When we look down on others or resent the authority of our managerial superiors, we find ourselves less positively disposed to cooperate with others, whether to help them or to call upon their help. Resentful and dismissive attitudes erode the spirit of solidarity. Managers need to ask themselves whether they cultivate good relations with employees, who can in turn help managers should the need arise. Employees should be seeking to build up a store of good will among co-workers, including bosses. Reciprocity fosters solidarity and mutual support.

The Parable of the Good Samaritan reminds us that a reversal of fortunes is an ever present, though unpredictable, possibility. External forces can do little to help in such times—despite the fact that we live in a world carried away with the idea of the social-assistance state or welfare state and within a political culture that sees itself as able to rescue everyone from poverty, sickness, disease, and high medical bills. The modern state has increasingly supplanted the Good Samaritan, and with that the ultimate knowledge that comes from a personal encounter with the vulnerable disappears as well. Increasing numbers of people have come to believe that they are discharging their moral obligations to their neighbor simply by paying taxes, voting for social assistance programs, or advocating for policy proposals to build a robust political apparatus. An entire organization operating under the name Bread for the World, despite its name, produces no loaves of bread for the hungry. It is little more than a political lobbying group. To what extent does this outsourcing of charity erode the cultural sense of responsibility and solidarity? Whatever arguments there may be for such bureaucratic and political systems of social service, it is amazing to see this parable employed to argue for the welfare state, on the supposition that it follows from—or even fulfills—Jesus' teaching.

Pope Francis offers a reflection on this parable in his social encyclical *Fratelli tutti*, and while he would be more comfortable with more political support than I in assisting the poor, he nonetheless points to the need for a more intimate and personal level of support in the face of human vulnerability.

He observes that the Samaritan offered the victim more than material support: "He also gave him something that in our frenetic world we cling to tightly: he gave him his time. Certainly, he had his own plans for that day, his own needs, commitments and desires. Yet he was able to put all that aside when confronted with someone in need. Without even knowing the injured man, he saw him as deserving of his time and attention."

We will be able "to direct society to the pursuit of the common good" as the pope put it, only by the interior disposition the pope so movingly describes—not by mere abstractions either initiated or dominated by the political order, but rather by creating a political and social order *out of the moral disposition of the Samaritan*. This is precisely the pope's point: "The parable clearly does not indulge in abstract moralizing, nor is its message merely social and ethical. It speaks to us of an essential and often forgotten aspect of our common humanity: we were created for a fulfilment that can only be found in love."[4]

To say that people are morally obliged to help those in need is not the same as to say that government action and public policy should be the *first* and *normative* way they are helped. Is voting or lobbying for political action and government benefits essentially what it means to be a Samaritan? Government welfare payments create dependencies that justify ever-higher spending, vast waste, and the pain and suffering that come with the taxation and control necessary to enable those things. The welfare state is by its very nature connected to vote-buying schemes and fraud. Welfare programs foster dishonesty on the part of the officeholders who pass them into law, the government employees who implement them, and the program beneficiaries. All of this is on top of the fact that distant impersonal bureaucracies simply do not know what the real human needs are on the ground in local communities, in human hearts, and in homes. This problem becomes exponentially worse as the size and activity of the political sphere grows.

Pope Benedict XVI (now emeritus) wrote in his first encyclical *Deus caritas est*, "The State which would provide everything, absorbing everything into itself, would ultimately become a mere bureaucracy incapable of guaranteeing the very thing which the suffering person—every person—needs: namely, loving personal concern. We do not need a State which regulates and controls everything, but a State which, in accordance with the principle of subsidiarity, generously acknowledges and supports initiatives arising from the different social forces and combines spontaneity with closeness to those in need."[5]

The opening of our parable—"A certain man went down from Jerusalem to Jericho, and fell among thieves, which stripped him of his raiment, and wounded him, and departed, leaving him half dead"—describes criminals very accurately. They often disregard the properties and liberties of others. It is a dangerous leap of faith and logic to suggest that the role of the Samaritan be absorbed by the state. To transfer such an obligation to a coercive apparatus may seem to relieve us of certain responsibilities, or even to ensure that they are met, but in fact it introduces many grave moral hazards.

The Samaritan was manifestly not an agent of the state. He was a private individual with a moral sensibility. This is the model that Jesus holds up to his disciples. The Samaritan helped of his own volition, which is the basis of virtue. He was not acting as a public servant who was compensated for his service, but instead used his own money. This was a *personal* sacrifice of his own time and resources. His actions were not only good for the poor suffering soul on the road; they were good for himself as well. The consistent emphasis of the parable is on the Samaritan's personal engagement with the victim of the robbery, his proximity to the man, his tending personally to the wounds left in the man's body, and the use of his own means of transport—all in complete contradiction of any politicized interpretation of the parable. After all, the main point of the parable is not the needs of the victim. The main point is the compassionate action of the Samaritan, who on that account turns out to be the "neighbor" of the victim—tending to the man with his own clothing (surely he brought no bandages on this business trip) and with his own provisions (the oil and wine) transporting him "on his own beast," and not only paying the innkeeper (whom he undoubtedly knew from previous trips) for the man's lodging and care, but even going so far as to obligate himself to pay for any service that exceeded the deposit he put down. No, this is not political activism at work; this is love.

The case for the inadequacy of private charity is that it is undependable and also degrading to those who need help. The argument is that a political solution—some combination of generous government welfare payments, structural change of the economy, the redistribution of wealth—is the normative way to guarantee social provision. Yet this approach has its own problems. The first problem is that it underplays the social potency of a moral model. Abstractions are not compassion, and they rarely inspire compassionate commitments. At some level, state action is always force. It may be necessary at times of grave social crisis, as a temporary remedy. But even in such cases, sweeping interventions can cause bigger problems than the ones they are meant to solve. Any government action ought to be located at the level closest to the problem.[6] To the extent that centralized intervention usurps or replaces the role of mediating institutions at the local level, it disincentivizes and denies people the chance to exercise charity. In addition, while charity is something to be received with gratitude and often involves personal concern and help for improvement in the life of the needy person, state welfare creates an expected right and, even if unintentionally, results in a relationship of dependency. Further, substituting welfare for charity erodes a culture of solidarity and reciprocal concern.

"Whatsoever thou spendest more," said the Samaritan, "when I come again, I will repay thee." This, right here, is authentic generosity. This is charity. It is exercised by someone acting on his own response to moral formation and the need of another person. It is an instance of admirable moral sensitivity at work—authentic compassion of one human being for another. There is, and can be, no substitute for that. This is just one of the many wonderful lessons of this beautiful parable.

In writing about this parable, Pope Benedict XVI offers an insight to the truly radical nature of human goodness: "We do of course have material assistance to offer and we have to examine our own way of life. *But we always give too little when we just give material things…* the priest and the Levite might have passed by more out of fear than out of indifference. The risk of goodness is something we must relearn from within, but we can only do that if we ourselves are 'neighbors' from within, and if we then have an eye for the sort of service that is asked of us…" [emphasis added].[7]

CHAPTER 12

The Rich Man and Lazarus

"There was a certain rich man, which was clothed in purple and fine linen, and fared sumptuously every day: And there was a certain beggar named Lazarus, which was laid at his gate, full of sores, and desiring to be fed with the crumbs which fell from the rich man's table: moreover the dogs came and licked his sores. And it came to pass, that the beggar died, and was carried by the angels into Abraham's bosom: the rich man also died, and was buried. And in hell he lift up his eyes, being in torments, and seeth Abraham afar off, and Lazarus in his bosom. And he cried and said, Father Abraham, have mercy on me, and send Lazarus, that he may dip the tip of his finger in water, and cool my tongue; for I am tormented in this flame. But Abraham said, Son, remember that thou in thy lifetime receivedst thy good things, and likewise Lazarus evil things: but now he is comforted, and thou art tormented. And beside all this, between us and you there is a great gulf fixed: so that they which would pass from hence to you cannot; neither can they pass to us, that would come from thence. Then he said, I pray thee therefore, father, that thou wouldest send him to my father's house: for I have five brethren; that he may testify unto them, lest they also come into this place of torment. Abraham saith unto him, They have Moses and the prophets; let them hear them. And he said, Nay, father Abraham: but if one went unto them from the dead, they will repent. And he said unto him, If they hear not Moses and the prophets, neither will they be persuaded, though one rose from the dead." (Luke 16:19–31)

T he theme of this parable is the fleeting nature of earthly goods and the reversal of fortunes. A rich man is portrayed as having had resources on earth that he did not employ well. Rather than demonstrating gratitude and generosity for his blessings, he displayed no pity for the poor and sick Lazarus. The rich man's real error is *not* that he actively harmed Lazarus, but that he never helped him, indeed, he never seemed to even notice him in this life. The reversal of fortunes comes in the afterlife, where the rich man suffers torments in Hades. Lazarus, who experiences a reversal of fortunes of another kind, is carried into the afterlife by angels and placed at the bosom of Abraham. The scene and the story are nothing short of terrifying, all the more poignantly so when the rich man in hell pleads for a drop of water from Lazarus.

To deepen our appreciation of this parable's confrontation with the question of wealth and poverty we will need to see it against the backdrop of what precedes it in the sixteenth chapter of Luke's Gospel, specifically verses 9–13. In these verses we hear Jesus' explanation of the Parable of the Unjust Steward, discussed previously in chapter 10, where Jesus connects wealth to the responsibility, honesty, and prudence that must accompany it. Only when we come to see wealth as opportunity can we really appreciate that neither its possession nor its absence confers moral status—but rather its use in a way that reveals the real character of the person using it.

An analogy can help us to see this point more clearly: A beautiful woman might be said to possess the *potential* for greater sexual immorality because a greater number of opportunities for licentiousness arise for her, in comparison to the opportunities that a less attractive person has. Are all beautiful women, therefore, intrinsically immoral? Obviously not. And neither are all rich people.

God's judgement of our lives is exacting in a way no human judgment could ever be. Before the face of God, every fact, every detail, every motive or intention is fully known and thoroughly understood. For almost everyone on earth, throughout all documented history, money has meant power. It is a path to fame, friends, indulgence, and license. It affords opportunity for greed and abuse of power. This has been true under every political system ever constructed. The rich are often envied and are sometimes annihilated. Still, it is rare to find a society in which the rich would gladly change places with the poor. Yet, that is exactly what is portrayed here, in the only parable actually set in the afterlife. In the Parable of the Rich Man and Lazarus, we are reminded of how things might easily be switched, and how our ultimate fate depends on our choices.

The contrasts between these two men in this life could not be starker—they differ in virtually everything: habitation, apparel, nourishment, general vulnerability.

The rich man lives in luxury, eats well, and lives behind gates. While much of the middle class lives this way today, this was a rare luxury in the ancient world, where most people struggled to survive the day. The pre-industrial age saw struggle, insecurity, and suffering as the norm for virtually everyone. The contrast could induce the few very rich to believe that they had reason for pride and being exalted above others.

The Parable of the Rich Man and Lazarus by Gustave Doré. *Project Gutenberg*

When reading about any rich person in the Bible, it is helpful to remember that despite the fact that trade was ubiquitous at the time, the rich in the ancient world did not become wealthy through trade. Before extensive trading networks were established in the Renaissance, people more usually became rich as a result of connections with the regime, either as members of a favored class holding power, as employees of the regime, as monopolists, or by inheriting wealth from ancestors in one of those categories. But however the rich man gained his wealth, the fact that he is rich is practically the only thing we are told about him—as the poverty of Lazarus is virtually all we know about him. This forces us to focus on the relationship between the two men's statuses in life and their eternal rewards. Was the rich man damned for his wealth, or for some sin to which his wealth tempted him? And more generally, what are the temptations and moral disadvantages and advantages to wealth and poverty?

We are told that the rich man dressed in purple and linen. The color and material here indicate great wealth, influence, or royalty—given the expense and difficulty of producing the dye needed for the color purple—suggesting the power he had over men. Perhaps even that he held some political post. We are given nothing concrete in the text as such.

Lazarus was at the polar opposite. He was poor and sick. Dogs licked his sores—whether in a friendly way or as scavengers seeking food. The image is of a degraded condition.[1] He was hungry and lay outside the gates. The gates themselves are a symbol of the utter and complete separation and exclusion of Lazarus from a protected, comfortable, or sheltered life—as well as a foreshadowing of the terrifying reversal later in the story. No mention is made of Lazarus' burial; we are left to wonder if he even had anyone willing to bear the expense on his behalf.

The Rich Man in Hell, Seeing Lazarus Embraced by Abraham by Heinrich Aldegrever.
Metropolitan Museum of Art

Yet both men die. Whereas poor Lazarus once begged from the rich man, the rich man now begs from Lazarus, and not even for a morsel of food but merely for a drop of water.

The story is very subtle throughout, conveying an almost subliminal message about the rich man's culpability vis-à-vis Lazarus' condition. That very subtlety can leave room for ideological agendas to be read into the parable.

One example of this comes from the late Ernesto Cardenal, a Catholic priest who was a prominent proponent of liberation theology in Nicaragua in the 1970s and 1980s and who served as the minister of culture under the Sandinistas for almost a decade. Father Cardenal was instrumental in forming a commune on Lake Nicaragua called Solentiname, where the poor were invited to comment on the Scriptures. Cardenal inserts a zero-sum economic assumption into his exegesis of the Parable of the Rich Man and Lazarus: "the poor man is badly off because the rich man is well off, or the rich man is better off because the poor man is badly off. There are poor people because there are rich people. And rich people's parties are at the cost of the poor people."[2]

But this is sheer invention. It overlooks the subtle indicators of the rich man's arrogance—which have nothing to do with a Marxist economic reading of the text.

Note that while the names of the wealthy are usually the ones that are known, in this story it is the poor man—Lazarus—who is named, and the rich man who goes nameless. Even in the midst of his torments we find the rich man giving Lazarus tasks to perform (to go to his brothers), while Lazarus utters not a sentence in the entire account.

The cosmic tables have been finally and unalterably turned. Where their earthly lots were temporary, their fates are now eternal. The rich man is far worse off in Hades than the poor man ever was in his temporal existence.

The spiritual implications are straightforward—if shocking. Are there any economic lessons to be learned? These are more complicated than it might first appear. One implication might be a warning to the rich not to be pompous—a theme found throughout Scripture, where the arrogance of the wealthy and powerful, rather than their mere riches, is often condemned. Economic standing is distinct from moral standing, as we see for instance in the example of Joseph of Arimathea, whose resources, placed at the service of Christ, are viewed favorably in the Gospels (see Matthew 27:57, Mark 15:43–46, and John 19:38).

The fleeting nature of wealth is something that commercial society itself underscores in its daily workings. In a system of feudalism or mercantilist privilege, where wealth is obtained and secured by connections to power, wealth may be secure in this. But those who have obtained riches by voluntary exchange and entrepreneurship should know that their wealth is vulnerable to the same market forces that produced it in the first place. They should know not to think of themselves as royalty, as people with power over others, because, in fact, they do not exercise raw power—that is, the right to wield the sword. The basis of their economic success is the ability to persuade people to engage in commerce for reciprocal benefit. In a market economy, you become rich by *serving*, not ruling, others.

Those who are successful in a market economy succeed primarily by employing their entrepreneurial judgment to serve others by offering them products at attractive prices. Their wealth is both the result and token of the service they render others through voluntary exchange. It is true that this yields profit, but this is nothing other than an indicator of their successful anticipation of the needs of others. It is for this reason that there is nothing immoral about profits as such. However, success in a market can tempt one to over-confidence and blind a person to a greater reality. This is a dangerous psychological and spiritual ailment that cannot only damage a person's soul, but can cause riches to evaporate as quickly as they came.

In a rivalrous market, it doesn't take long for a firm to lose market share. The rich rarely stay that way longer than a generation or two. One cannot rest on one's laurels: there are no guarantees. The conditions that lead to success can easily change. Wealth in a market economy is dynamic because to be "rich" is a reversible condition, as any perusal of the various lists of the wealthiest will demonstrate from year to year.[3]

These are facts that any entrepreneur knows well. Once someone in business ceases to think of him or herself as a servant of others and begins instead to think of himself as somehow entitled to his status, as the rich man in the parable does, he endangers all he has. This parable thus not only forecasts our eternal destinies, it reflects reality in the here and now as well.

Simply put, this parable is a warning to the complacent and myopic rich. Not only is it a warning to avoid attachments to earthly goods, it is also an admonishment that to be successful ethically requires an other-directedness and outward gaze, a concern for those around us. The fact that the rich man knew Lazarus' name yet did nothing to relieve his distress shows he lacked the mind of a servant. Service, charity, and humility are the characteristics that mark the authentic servant of God. You might say that pride in riches goes before a big fall—including, at times, a fall in cash balances.

Think of the rich in the late 1920s—or, more recently, of the dot-com rich before the crash of the internet commercial sector in the late 1990s. In more recent memory, there were the large financial companies of the late 2000s who held enormous portfolios of securitized mortgages, based on the presumption that housing prices would never stop rising. One has the impression that these investors believed they could never make a bad decision. But the market humbles as well as exalts. It can reduce a man from riches to rags in a shockingly swift period of time. We prepare for this not by stockpiling or becoming miserly, but by adopting an attitude of gratitude and prayerful respect for others and by not thinking of economic success as the *summum bonum* of our existence.

There is indeed a grave and eternal danger in donning the purple and feasting while others around us are in pain and hunger. Even if there is no cause and effect between the two, by behaving in this way we are acquiescing to the temptation to forget our own mortality and vulnerability. This is who the rich man really is, and his fate can be a sober reminder. It does not have to be our fate. Looking to Lazarus' final destination, we can act in ways to make it our own.

CHAPTER 13

The Prodigal Son

"And he said, A certain man had two sons: And the younger of them said to his father, Father, give me the portion of goods that falleth to me. And he divided unto them his living. And not many days after the younger son gathered all together, and took his journey into a far country, and there wasted his substance with riotous living. And when he had spent all, there arose a mighty famine in that land; and he began to be in want. And he went and joined himself to a citizen of that country; and he sent him into his fields to feed swine. And he would fain have filled his belly with the husks that the swine did eat: and no man gave unto him. And when he came to himself, he said, How many hired servants of my father's have bread enough and to spare, and I perish with hunger! I will arise and go to my father, and will say unto him, Father, I have sinned against heaven, and before thee, And am no more worthy to be called thy son: make me as one of thy hired servants. And he arose, and came to his father. But when he was yet a great way off, his father saw him, and had compassion, and ran, and fell on his neck, and kissed him. And the son said unto him, Father,

The Prodigal Son amid the Swine by Albrecht Dürer. *Rijksmuseum*

I have sinned against heaven, and in thy sight, and am no more worthy to be called thy son. But the father said to his servants, Bring forth the best robe, and put it on him; and put a ring on his hand, and shoes on his feet: And bring hither the fatted calf, and kill it; and let us eat, and be merry: For this my son was dead, and is alive again; he was lost, and is found. And they began to be merry. Now his elder son was in the field: and as he came and drew nigh to the house, he heard musick and dancing. And he called one of the servants, and asked what these things meant. And he said unto him, Thy brother is come; and thy father hath killed the fatted calf, because he hath received him safe and sound. And he was angry, and would not go in: therefore came his father out, and intreated him. And he answering said to his father, Lo, these many years do I serve thee, neither transgressed I at any time thy commandment: and yet thou never gavest me a kid, that I might make merry with my friends: But as soon as this thy son was come, which hath devoured thy living with harlots, thou hast killed for him the fatted calf. And he said unto him, Son, thou art ever with me, and all that I have is thine. It was meet that we should make merry, and be glad: for this thy brother was dead, and is alive again; and was lost, and is found." (Luke 15:11–32)

Arguably the best known, and certainly lengthiest of all of Jesus' parables, the Prodigal Son is the one most depicted in artistic renderings. Over the centuries, this story has immediately drawn people in. What makes it so compelling? We can

The Return of the Prodigal Son by Gustave Doré. Bible Gallery

easily recognize our own experiences in the arc of this story, and we identify with the iconic characters, so expertly depicted.

The two sons are different in some distinct ways, but surprisingly similar in other fundamentals. Despite the fact that the title by which we know the parable names the younger, wayward son, the real axis of this story is the person of the father. Its main themes and intersecting points of interest arise from his relationship with his two sons.

In our study of Jesus' parables we have sought to fill in gaps related to their economic presuppositions and ramifications rather than attempting to offer a comprehensive analysis of the parables in all their amazing and intriguing detail. The broader theological, soteriological, and even eschatological implications have not been our focus, except to the extent to which they throw light on our more proscribed and focused project of economics.

Economics, which is the sphere of human action related to easing people's want, involves efforts to secure one's future—including commerce, productivity, risk-taking, contracts and guarantees of their integrity, and rights of inheritance. This parable touches on all these subjects. Other major themes of the parable are covetousness and jealousy, forgiveness, freedom, fairness, justice, charity, and how the way we value material goods affects our relationships, even our intimate ones.

While the "economic elements" of the Parable of the Prodigal Son "can, perhaps, be seen as incidental and dispensable to the intention of the parable"—certainly, they are not the main moral or theological lesson imparted—they give us a way into a deeper moral understanding of the parable and can only enhance our understanding or appreciation of the story in all its dimensions.[1] In this sense, the story of the prodigal son is very much like the story of the Incarnation itself: the comingling of divine transcendence with the human contingency. Or to put it in a word, Emmanuel (God-with-us).

In addition to the economic—and cultural, linguistic, and social—background of any parable, it is also good to keep in mind that a parable remains a story in its own right, with its own goal and purpose (admittedly sometimes not so easy to discern). Thus our exploration cannot be confined to a study of the laws or customs of an era—a temptation that some commentators and homilists can fall into. A parable works as a story to teach a message all on its own. We must not be absorbed by the cultural context in which the story takes place at the expense of the lesson of the parable itself.

The story begins with a young man who yields to the lure of unrestrained liberty by obtaining an inheritance that he ends up squandering, bringing himself to a desperate state. One has the impression that he is the naïve member of the family who exhibits the classic trait of selfish immaturity. As a result of his own ineptitude or blind ambition, he must confront deprivation and want. He finds himself miserable but also deeply reflective and honest.

It is in this situation that he speaks of his offense against his father in demanding his inheritance early and wasting it. He describes what he has done as a sin, both against his father and "against heaven." This sin, which involves obtaining and wasting material resources the younger son obviously covets, has moral and economic dimensions. More poignantly, it reveals a disregard for his father.

As the story unfolds, we learn that this young man has an older brother very different from himself. Whereas the younger sibling abandons his father, his family, and his responsibilities, his older brother remains loyally at home and is seen laboring late into the day to maintain and help manage the family estate. Yet as the drama continues, we will see that the older brother's attitude toward his father—in particular his resentfulness—has something in common with the younger brother's material preoccupation.

From the economic—or at least the material—point of view, the younger brother is an imprudent and unsuccessful prodigal. He wastes his inheritance and reduces himself to near starvation. The older brother, in contrast, is a prudent and industrious contributor to the success of the family estate. He exhibits the willingness to forgo consumption that, as we have seen, is a necessary condition for success in business. And his self-control is rewarded with success—on the material plane. But while the two brothers are polar opposites with respect to the economic aspects of life, both of them, in different ways and at different point in the story, fail at something that is more important than economics. Ironically, both of them—the wastrel who prodigally dissipates his inheritance and ruins himself, and the self-denying, industrious, responsible, successful man—fall into the mistake of making material goods the most important value. The younger brother values those goods for the pleasures they allow him to enjoy. The older brother values them for the status and self-worth they give him. But both brothers allow the value of those material goods to obscure the infinitely greater value of their relationships to their father, and to each other.

It is not difficult to imagine how the young brother felt. He has his whole life ahead of him and can hardly wait to make his mark in the world, but he finds himself bound to the drudgery of a family farm. What child doesn't want to break free from time to time? The quest for freedom is deep in our DNA. We desire to experience a life unrestrained by any boundaries, without anyone to inhibit our passions, to pursue our bliss without anything to get in the way of our enthusiasms. For many, this is the very definition of liberty: no boundaries.

We need go no further than the words spoken by the now-disgraced movie producer Harvey Weinstein, who offered an explanation for his longtime sexual habit of exploiting women. He said that he had come of age "in the 60's and 70's, when all the rules about behavior and workplaces were different." What he meant by this is something that any of us who lived through this period will remember. (The rest of you can just Google clips of Woodstock). At that time the zeitgeist urged people to enter fully into their passions, casting aside the outdated strictures of tradition and religious restraints that were thought only to inhibit human fulfillment. The argument was then, and in many places still is now, that the only way to discover who you really are is to follow where your passions lead.

One senses a similar impulse in the mind of the prodigal son as he severs ties to his family. But the ramifications of such a notion of liberty are as evident as a hangover.

How satisfying is it to just randomly toss or kick a ball around a field with some friends? It can be fun for a time. But it doesn't yield the same kind of exhilaration as overcoming obstacles and challenges, mastering skills, playing by the rules, and winning actual games in a sport. That deep sense of accomplishment and fruition can be achieved only within the confines of the rules of, say baseball or soccer, when goals are achieved and obstacles are surmounted. The thrill of victory is made possible by the rules that form the very definition of the game. A frame, after all, needn't diminish a beautiful scene; it can focus our eye on its beauty or highlight a detail that would otherwise go unseen. Liberty has no meaning unless it is directed to some higher goal or truth.

The Parable of the Prodigal Son begins with inheritance and the role it plays in family dynamics. The tensions created by the interplay between personal relationships—especially longstanding and intimate personal relationships—and financial considerations give depth and drama to the story and the lessons we will learn from it. Issues of possessions, money, and inheritance are the backdrop to the entire story—without them, it would lose its meaning.

Klyne Snodgrass, a renowned scholar of the parables, observes that scholars are divided on whether a request (or demand) of the kind the younger son makes to his father was common or not. Receiving an early inheritance was not unknown in this period, but to ask to receive one's inheritance prior to the death of a father would imply insolence—and at the very least betray that the son was more interested in the money than in his father or his family's legacy.[2]

The core concern here—and in other places throughout the Gospels, as we have seen, is really not about money *as such* as much as it is about people's attitude toward money, and how that attitude affects their relationships with other human beings, and with God.

It is this human factor that ought to distinguish economics, properly conceived, from mere mathematical calculations, abstractions, considerations of profit and loss, and a preoccupation with material goods. The Prodigal Son is the third in a series of parables in this section of Luke that present us with things that are lost and then found. The two others are about a sheep and a coin—entities that lack reason, free will, and moral responsibility, so that they exist on an entirely different plane from the two sons. The sheep who wandered off (Luke 15:3–7) is vulnerable, but cannot be said to be either guilty or innocent; likewise, the misplaced coin (Luke 8:10) may cause anxiety to the woman who lost it, and its recovery prompts her to throw a party, but the coin didn't lose any sleep over being lost. It is the human capacity to reason, which enables people to live meaningfully and productively in this world, that also gives moral dimension to our actions and enables us to set value on things. It is only human beings who reason and thus can value and make choices, as inanimate objects and animals cannot. In these parables, we are keenly aware that the focus is not so much on the sheep as on the rescue by the shepherd, or on the coin as on the woman. While neither the coin nor the sheep has a point of view worth considering, the prodigal is a moral actor—as are his father and his brother.

The moral actions, consequences, and lessons revealed in the decisions of other people involve us in their stories. And it is especially easy for us to feel a connection to this story. Our awareness of our own capacity to betray our deepest values and our hopes for restoration and forgiveness make the Parable of the Prodigal Son compelling. We are prompted by the actions of both sons to assess our own lives in moral terms. The character of the father, revealed in the manner in which he relates to both his sons, lifts our eyes to show us how to approach the economic circumstances of our lives in a way that transcends the mere materiality of our existence. It is the family and their relationships that he holds as his highest value.

This parable—especially the reaction of the elder brother to the news of his young sibling's return—raises the question of fairness.

The Return of the Prodigal Son by Rembrandt. *Metropolitan Museum of Art*

One suspects that there may have been tensions between the brothers before this incident. After all, sibling rivalry is hardly unknown in human history. It appeared on the scene with Cain and Abel (Genesis 4), and it has remained a constant in human experience ever since. We see it in the Scriptures with Isaac and Ishmael in Genesis 16; and Jacob and Esau in Genesis 25, 28, 32, and 33; and Joseph and his brothers in Genesis 37. We see it in the classical world, in Romulus and Remus and in Cleopatra and Ptolemy XIII. In our modern world it exists in entertainment (Olivia de Havilland and Joan Fontaine) and sports (brothers and NFL coaches Jim and John Harbaugh). Sometimes the closer people are, the deeper the tensions.

Entire family fortunes have been ruined by rivalry, greed, jealousy, resentment, and perceptions of favoritism (sometime long buried). The best-known fictional exploration of the phenomenon is *Bleak House* by Charles Dickens, a labyrinthine novel recounting in elaborate detail the dissipation of a family fortune. It paints a sad picture of the epic saga of the unwinding of an enormous multigenerational estate as the result of family members' resentments, litigiousness, personal foibles, and secrets. It is sobering to contemplate how many family fortunes have been lost to the inability to achieve some kind of reconciliation.

Families, however, are bound together by more than the material goods that they share and contend over. They are bound as well by blood, culture and, one hopes, love—which is just what the father in the Parable of the Prodigal Son demonstrates *to both of his sons.*

The sons in the parable find themselves alienated from one another and their father precisely because they—each in his own way—prioritize material things above their familial bonds. This is most obvious in the younger son's demand for his inheritance *before his father is dead.* Yet we detect a similar discontentment on the part of his older brother as the result of a very similar attitude. While it appears that he has never lacked for anything, he sees himself as underappreciated: he clearly feels that his younger brother is held in higher esteem and indulged as he never has been, despite having always stayed at home laboring for his father: "And he was angry, and would not go in: therefore came his father out, and intreated him. And he answering said to his father, Lo, these many years do I serve thee, neither transgressed I at any time thy commandment: and yet thou never gavest me a kid, that I might make merry with my friends: But as soon as this thy son was come, which hath devoured thy living with harlots, thou hast killed for him the fatted calf" (Luke 15:28–30). The father never sees it that way at all, as is evident when he tells his older son that "all that I have is thine" (Luke 15:31) and immediately shifts the focus from the material to the personal: "for this thy brother was dead, and is alive again; and was lost, and is found" (Luke 15:32).

The younger brother's waywardness seems to have brought the older brother's resentment to the surface—though neither he nor their father appears to have had his lifestyle diminished as a result. Something is keeping the older son from making use of what he has in a satisfying way. This is another important thing to contemplate from this parable: Is resentment preventing us from being happy, even when all our material needs are satisfied?

The older son finds himself outside his father's orbit because he has chosen to place himself there. He is, in effect, now in the place his younger brother once occupied. If he "came to himself," overcame the momentary humiliation and pain of entering into the banquet, and was reconciled to his brother, he would have experienced a healing like the younger brother's homecoming was for him.

How sad it must be for this loving a father to provide so generous a welcome to his one son "who was lost but is now found, who was dead but now is alive," only to have his other son not warm to this outreach and himself become lost, alienated, dead.

It is easy to see the elder brother as an immature, pouting baby. "Get over it," we may want to yell at him. But for a moment let's look at the situation through his eyes, even if in the end we see that his perspective is lacking.

Here is a man who grew up at a time and in a culture where the eldest son was held in a position of high esteem. According to Deuteronomy 21:17, the eldest son was to inherit a double portion of the estate. This would mean that whatever the amount of the inheritance the younger brother dissipated, the elder brother could still expect a two-thirds share of the estate. Nor do he and his father appear to be in dire straits, given the father's ability to throw an evidently impressive celebration.

Even with no knowledge of earlier causes for the sibling rivalry with his brother, his brother's abandonment of his responsibilities—no doubt adding to his own—is in itself insulting and probably burdensome. And the wrong is only compounded by the fact of his taking a share of the family estate, which understandably adds to the grievance. Material things—and our presumed entitlement to them—can blind us to things of higher import. But all too often, when considering spiritual and moral questions, good people can miss the intricate and overlapping ways in which possessions and material things connect to transcendent matters such as family, moral choices, and virtue.

This parable offers lessons in justice and the right ordering of inheritances. And certainly, fairness is essential to maintaining right order in social relations. Fairness, or justice, demands that we treat people as they deserve to be treated, and that is a necessary condition for social cohesion.

But the story goes deeper. What we have before our eyes is much more than a lesson in fairness, or in the right ordering of an inheritance.[3] In reading this story we are learning something more subtle than merely a lesson in justice, in what people deserve; we are learning about mercy—which exceeds justice. And yet mercy requires the notion of justice, because without understanding justice we are unable to see the transformative power of mercy. The power of mercy is difficult to see if there is no understanding of justice in the first place. This is why it is so dangerous either to separate the two or to reduce everything to a right, to a claim of justice. To do so eviscerates love and charity. People can *demand* justice because it is their right; they can only *plead* for mercy. Both sons initially demand justice. The younger will eventually plead for mercy, and his father will shower it on him. We're left wondering whether the older son will show the same mercy.

The reason that this story goes deeper than justice is that the father pushes it deeper as he relates to both his sons. The offer of a second chance to the younger son is made all the more compelling by the fact that the reprieve is being offered by the offended party, the father. The father's acceptance of his younger son's turnaround captivates us. We are drawn in by his eagerness to reconcile with his son and restore him to his previous status, which is seen in his running to greet his son even before a word is spoken between them (Luke 15:20).

As Professor Snodgrass points out, the forgiveness the father offers the son in the face of his self-centeredness is predicated more on the character and generosity of the father than on the perfect repentance of his son. The son never even finishes his confession.[4] Truly the character of the patriarch in this story is as compelling as the role of the Prodigal himself. In one sense, this is really the Parable of the Loving Father.

This is the obvious emotional heart of the story: the idea that even after the younger son's insolent demand for his inheritance, and the abject failure to which his greed and ambition lead him, the father (unlike his older son) appears to hold no grudge, but seizes the initiative and runs to embrace his son with love, discarding his status as the aggrieved party—and then in the same way, he is willing to go out of the banquet to entreat his older son to come inside.

We have all been wronged. Depending on the dynamics of the relationship and the depth of the betrayal, we are likely to think it only decent that prior to reestablishing the relationship, that at least the situation should be clarified, cards put on the table, restitution made, and an apology proffered by the offending party. We teach children at an early age that offering and receiving apologies is the right and proper thing to do. But even in the face of a sincere apology, many find it almost constitutionally impossible to get beyond the offense, especially if the wrong was deep. Sometimes it is a matter of moving gradually and letting go of the pain piece by piece. Christ's command to his disciples to forgive everyone who sinned against them—"if ye forgive not men their trespasses, neither will your Father forgive your trespasses" (Matthew 6:15)—is admittedly one of the most difficult demands of Christianity. Even in my solidly Catholic Italian-American family, we used to joke about "Italian Alzheimer's"—defined as when you forget everything but the grudge.

The kind, gentle, and generous nature of the father juxtaposed to the selfishness of his sons is the gravamen of the parable.[5] The image of a wronged father emerging with joy at the sight of his offending son, not even yet knowing the purpose of the son's appearance, has great effect in communicating the love of God toward his children, even when, or especially when, they betray him.

Even at his lowest point, something remained in the Prodigal that made him capable of recalling his real identity, coming to himself, and deciding to put things right. The essential thing we can take away from this story is a model of love and grace, but not ideals abstracted from the daily lives of real human beings. All this occurs in the context of mundane questions of rights and property, hurt feelings, and potential resentments. It is a world very much like the one we live in. The father's reconciling love for his son radiates throughout the contingencies of risk, ambition, and failure.

The Parable of the Prodigal Son ends with celebration. Celebrations can be superficial, even debauched—as for example the younger son's dissipation in the far-off country, when he "waste[s] his substance with riotous living." There are places in Luke's Gospel where "to celebrate"—*euphrainein* in the Greek—has negative connotations. Remember, for example the Rich Fool who said to himself, "Soul, thou hast much goods laid up for many years; take thine ease, eat, drink, and be merry [*euphrainou*] (Luke 12:19)," and also the Rich

Man, who "was clothed in purple and fine linen, and fared sumptuously [*euphrainomenos*] every day" while Lazarus was lying at his
gate "full of sores" (Luke 16:19–20). But in the Parable of the Prodigal
Son the same word for celebrating is employed positively: "But the
father said to his servants, Bring forth the best robe, and put it on
him; and put a ring on his hand, and shoes on his feet: And bring
hither the fatted calf, and kill it; and let us eat, and be merry: For this
my son was dead, and is alive again; he was lost, and is found. And
they began to be merry [*euphrainesthai*]" (Luke 15:22–24).[6]

It is a joyful note to end a story that could have had a very different conclusion.

Some Broader Thoughts on Economics and the New Testament

E conomic matters pervade practically the whole of human life on earth; by virtue of our material existence, we find ourselves in the context of scarcity and limitation. Our physical natures and limitations give rise to the necessity of work. In calling the universe into being, God himself is seen to be working, and then entrusts the newly created human family with a vocation to do likewise (see Genesis 1:28). Our physicality gives rise to what today we call "economics," the search for the best and most prudent and efficient employment of scarce resources. What we term "the market" is not, then, a place, but a process of discovery of how to use these scarce and limited resources.

Yet this corporeal reality and this process of discovering how to live better rooted in our natural world—with less waste and greater efficiency—is not the goal of the human person, and does not define human life in its totality. The fact that we have been made of the "dust of the earth" gives rise to these contingencies, but human beings also have breathed into them "the breath of life." Thus matters related to the economy—poverty, property, wealth, money, profit, waste, inheritance, contracts, labor relations and the like—must all be considered in *both* their material and transcendent dimensions. Jesus and the New Testament writers utilized these dimensions of human life in the parables both to take account of the economic reality that is an inescapable part of our life in this world, and for a higher aim.

The primary focus of this book is on parables that exemplify these connections, and it does not even examine all of them. Depending on the precise definition of what constitutes a parable, there are estimated to be between one and two hundred of them contained within the New Testament. Here I have chosen a mere baker's dozen of the more familiar of Jesus' parables.

In studying how the Scriptures and economics interrelate, it is good to remember that the formal systematic or "scientific" study of the use of scarce resources as an intellectual discipline would emerge only gradually over time; it was unknown, as such, in the ancient world. It would be anomalous to speak of New Testament "economics" as though there were formal schools of economic thought in the ancient world.

What we mean today by economics was simply not in the minds of the biblical writers. When they used the word οἶκος and νέμομαι, the ancients intended only household management. The term for "economics" derived from those two Greek words, was formulated to connote the modern and more broad understanding of economics only under the influence of scholastic theologians and moral philosophers such as Juan de Mariana (1536–1624), Francisco de Vitoria (c. 1485–1546), Martín de Azpilcueta Navarrus (c. 1493–1586), Diego de Covarrubias y Leiva (1512–1577), among many others of the late scholastic school, all students and carriers of the Thomistic tradition of thought.[1]

The moral principles laid down in the teaching of Christ and his apostles form the values system out of which believers make economic choices, but this ought not to be conflated with any notion of "Biblical economics" per se. And yet one can say that the values of the Bible, the Christian way of viewing the world and humanity's place in the world, did influence the very development of economics as an intellectual discipline.

In this afterword I propose to address a number of the tensions found more generally in the New Testament, exercising the same effort to avoid bringing to the text my own set of presuppositions as when I approached the parables in the chapters of this book. I am still asking questions drawn from what I know of economics and attempting to connect the established principles of that field of economic science to the themes and encounters described in the pages of the New Testament.

One finds numerous warnings throughout the New Testament—both from the mouth of Jesus and in the teachings of the apostles and evangelists—related to wealth or riches and the challenge that material prosperity can pose to the pursuit of Christian discipleship. From a Christian perspective, material abundance and prosperity can become a hindrance to what ought to be the goal of human life: union with God, or salvation.

While an entire book could be devoted to this topic (I refer you to my *Defending the Free Market: The Moral Case for a Free Economy*, published by Regnery in 2012), it is valuable to explore the principal texts in the New Testament that relate to wealth, prosperity, and business in order to gain a deeper understanding of what the Christian challenge is to the believer.

These texts are rich in instruction for radical and authentic discipleship. They are so rich in this regard that it is imperative that we permit the meaning of the text itself to speak to our hearts on its own terms, setting aside any propensity to rationalize their meaning so as to empty it of all challenge to us, but not beginning with the assumption that Jesus makes the renunciation of property a condition of discipleship, either.

Moral Questions about Private Property and Wealth

Some understanding of "mine" and "thine" is implicit in the commandment against stealing. Why is theft a sin if private property is immoral in the first instance? The reality of scarcity means that we cannot all be equal owners of all things; that is a physical impossibility. Even the concept of sharing (as opposed to expropriation) implies ownership and choice. Recognizing that God is the ultimate owner of all property, we still live with the reality of the need for individuals and organizations to exercise stewardship. As we have seen, the parables presume the existence and morality of private ownership, along with all that this implies about choice, trade, and markets.

What about work as it relates to property? In the Bible, the first image we have of humanity on earth is in a garden. When we juxtapose a garden with a jungle, we begin to see the indispensable role of human work in relation to the natural world. Man is called to "till" the garden, that is, to cultivate it. Human beings prune nature, arrange it, render it more productive and fruitful, more ordered and at times, even more beautiful than it would otherwise be. This engagement with the natural order bespeaks the empresarial action of God himself, out of whose imagination human beings were created. Today, even to touch or manipulate the natural environment is frowned upon by many. Genesis may not present us with a complete anthropological vision, but key elements at the outset of the biblical vision reflect a value for human productivity and creativity.

Some seem to find it difficult to apply those concepts to commerce, the creation of wealth, and other elements of economic life. But the same is true of the biblical view of sexuality, which we also find in Genesis: something that is intrinsic to our vocation, and that—if it is approached in the right way—both manifests and brings people closer to God.

From the moral viewpoint, wealth and a productive economy are like human sexuality in that they contain a deep tug toward something transcendent. Our passions and desires are part of our very natures because God has "put eternity into man's mind" (Ecclesiastes 3:11).[2] Because we all yearn for God to fulfill us, we are desiring beings. Christian anthropology sees the human person as created for God, in whom alone we can find our ultimate fulfillment and meaning. Saint Augustine puts it so beautifully in the opening chapter of *The Confessions* when he says, "For Thou hast made us for Thyself and our hearts are restless till they rest in Thee."[3]

When this tug toward transcendence becomes distorted or misdirected, it can cause us to seek fulfillment in things other than God, in effect making those things, such as wealth or sex, idols—that is, substitutes for our supreme and authentic good and proper end.

It is for this reason that Jesus warns that life's worries, riches, and other pleasures can be dangerous, as he explains in the Parable of the Sower: "And that which fell among thorns are they, which, when they have heard, go forth, and are choked with cares and riches and pleasures of this life, and bring no fruit to perfection" (Luke 7:5–15). Those cares, riches, and pleasures can cause us to justify acquisitiveness or disordinate passions. The apostle Paul makes a distinction between money itself and what he calls "the love of money," which he says is "the root of all evil: which while some coveted after, they have erred from the faith, and pierced themselves through with many sorrows" (1 Timothy 6:10). The love of money can in fact be subtly (and sometimes not so subtly) at the base of all varieties of evil. And Christians living in prosperous twenty-first-century economies can easily persuade themselves that such temptations do not apply to them. Holy Scripture warns of the spiritual dangers of wealth, much as it warns of the temptations of sex. Both can be good, but only when directed to their proper ends.

The biblical warnings about wealth are not warnings against own-ership as such but against possessiveness about things. These are distinct moral categories. Vices flow from a disordered relation to material things: loving them as one should a person, or even God himself; acquiring them through unjust means; lusting for them; depending on them instead of God; putting money above faith, morality, and people; treating money as an end in itself rather than as a means to a higher end; clinging to it. All these are disordinate and disproportionate relationships with our possessions.

On the other hand, ownership as a form or mode of stewardship that itself results from creativity is another matter altogether. Chris-tianity has never taught that wealth as such is evil but has warned, instead, against the vices of intemperance, over-indulgence, greed, and acquisitiveness. We see this in the traditional seven deadly sins which condemn as vices not money, but greed; not sex, but lust; not success, but pride; not admiration, but envy; not eating or enjoying food, but gluttony; not even indignation or anger, but wrath; and not leisure, but sloth.

Throughout history, devout and profound scholars and saints have elaborated on the proper balance, the pitfalls, and how to live a virtuous life with regard to wealth. The Christian antidote for the vices named above is not to be found in a large and redistributive state "helping" people to part with their sin by expropriating their money, but in the difficult cultivation of an interior life of virtues such as detachment from possession, simplicity of life, modesty, thrift, and generosity in all we do. We do not fight greed, much less attain virtue, by impoverishing people or expropriating their wealth, or in making the assumption that only the prosperous can be greedy. The achievement of virtue is not as simple as reducing everyone to poverty—a rather easy thing to accomplish, if you think about it.

And it is all too easy to speak as though the human relationship to wealth, success, and work is simple and clear cut. While on the one hand the pursuit of wealth in itself can ensnare us and obscure our moral sensibilities, on the other dedication to work can be the pursuit of fulfillment, or of excellence as a response to a vocation or even a sacred calling experienced interiorly.

In the fourth chapter of Philippians, Paul expresses some thoughts on how he has navigated this tension: "Not that I complain of want; for I have learned, in whatever state I am, to be content. I know how to be abased, and I know how to abound; in any and all circumstances I have learned the secret of facing plenty and hunger, abundance and want. I can do all things in him who strengthens me."[4]

What is this "secret" of which the apostle speaks? The Amplified Bible expounds on Paul's words: "I know how to get along and live humbly [in difficult times], and I also know how to enjoy abundance and live in prosperity. In any and every circumstance I have learned the secret [of facing life], whether well-fed or going hungry, whether having an abundance or being in need." The Apostle provides the key when he says: "I can do everything through him who gives me strength."[5]

This is not just a call to "grin and bear it"; it is, rather, an insight into how to live a life of contentment by possessing a rightly ordered value system, so that one is not distracted by, or caught up in, the context in which one finds oneself. It is to be content (not just to endure) abundance or poverty. Consider an analogy from the families of loved ones who live with addictions such as alcohol or drugs. They will often say that the key is "detachment"—that is, one's own identity and meaning outside of oneself and one's highest values. Detachment does not mean denying one's context, situation, or reality, but does mean refusing to be defined by it. It means cultivating a serene awareness of one's priorities and limits, stepping back from something destructive, not clinging. In the context of our focus on the question relating to "abundance and want," detachment is the ability to avoid becoming obsessed with material things. I like the phrase "handling things lightly." I once heard a highly accomplished man express the ideal attitude superbly. Rich DeVos, a man I came to call a friend in my adopted home of Grand Rapids, Michigan, once said that we must "hold our material possessions with an open hand, and not a closed fist." This image, conveyed by a billionaire, strikes me as exactly the right balance. It is the antithesis of hoarding and clutching things; it is a vision of generosity and interior freedom.

Wealth represents a potent attraction to our passions; it appeals to our desires to such a great extent that it can substitute for God. Wealth can eclipse every other value in our lives if our desire for it is left unchecked. In reality, this is the lure of any form of idolatry.

As we have seen, human sexuality is another aspect of human life where we see the same dynamic at play. In the Christian tradition, neither material things nor sexuality can be defined as intrinsically evil. An intrinsic evil is something that is sinful in itself: while murder (the intentional and unjust taking of human life) is morally unacceptable at all times, killing (the taking of human life), may not be, depending on circumstances such as just self-defense, or when the killing is unintended, as in the case of an accident. Likewise, we may ask whether human sexuality is expressed generously and faithfully, as in marriage, or if it is turned in on itself—in which case it becomes selfish, promiscuous, violent, exploitative, and gravely sinful. But when human sexuality meets the moral requirements of the natural law and the Scriptures, it becomes holy, and indeed, in my tradition at least, sacramental.

Distinctions between the moral and the immoral use of wealth are even more critical as the world itself becomes generally richer—and life improves for people who had previously existed at subsistence levels. Failing to make distinctions between right and wrong ways of handling abundant material goods means that the pursuit of virtue in these matters becomes more irrelevant, obscure, truncated, and abstract—reduced to platitudes and detached from anything concrete and reasonably attainable. Vague yearnings can too easily result in the perfect being the enemy of the good, rendering the virtuous life so completely out of reach that it becomes utopian, which literally means "nowhere." A truly virtuous use of this world's goods, in contrast, is the stuff of real sanctification, requiring constant vigilance: habits of prayer, moral reflection, accountability, and contemplation. Wealth can be seductive as a substitute for the transcendent, and the best way to combat such seduction is to contemplate the real thing.

Technology and the Wealth of Nations

The astonishing rise of the wealthy society over the last two hundred years—a tiny portion of human history—has completely changed our conception of what life on earth can be like. It has shifted our expectations about what is possible. It has allowed us to imagine and even take for granted the possibility of material progress and prosperity for the masses of people. The "great divergence" of the modern West from the norm of pre-industrial economies (and the rest of the world) began at the Industrial Revolution and continued through the great age of liberalism in the nineteenth century. The reason for the divergence is the subject of widespread debate among economists and historians. Was it institutional change, political change, technological change, or cultural change? The answer has theological ramifications.

There is no one easy answer to the question, and a complete picture probably requires a balanced understanding of the relationship among all of these factors. By themselves, history and statistics reveal nothing about cause and effect; causal factors can only be discerned through good theory. But note that there is a common feature that researchers in this area agree on: human well-being is inseparable from technological innovation and capital accumulation. What occurred in the period following the Industrial Revolution is the very definition of what it can mean to be responsible and faithful to the requirement of the gospel to care for the poor and vulnerable.

The fact is that between 1800 and 1950 the proportion of the world's population living in dire poverty was cut in half, and then it was cut in half again from 1950 to 1980.[6] An American farmer in 2000 "produced on average 12 times as much farm output per hour worked as a farmer did in 1950. The development of new technology was a primary factor in these improvements."[7]

There were environmental impacts: increased energy use—as, for example, the greater use of tractors—boosted greenhouse gas emissions, at least initially. But that is only part of the picture. Greater use of such farm machinery also increased productivity and thus fed more people. And the increase in emissions was itself mitigated by continued technological advances such as more fuel-efficient engines and alternative power sources.

But pollution and climate concerns aren't the only problems that arise in tandem with the technological revolution in farming that has allowed us to feed billions more human beings. Notice that this dramatic increase in human well-being has taken place in a way that is clearly and obviously *inequitable*. It is here that the potential for envy arises: the rich get richer to a greater and faster degree than the poor climb from poverty. And yet, as you observe the long-run trends, it is clear that rising wealth has benefitted the entire world community.

So here is the challenge: imagine a policy mandating that no progress would be allowed unless it could take place evenly across all countries and across all demographic groups at the same time. We could hold equality in the pace of progress as *the* moral priority. And that is the policy we should adopt if we believe that no one group should become prosperous unless all groups share equally in the blessings of rising prosperity. We could ensure equality—but only at the expense of long-run increases for human well-being in general.

Think of how under that rule the outcome of history would have been very different. It would mean that *as a world community*, we would be one tenth as wealthy as we are presently—and that people would live little more than half as long as they do at present. *I am speaking here about the whole world.* These are moral considerations we must face when prioritizing equality over the freedom to create and own resources. Consider, too, an additional fact related to the size of the world population, which is now seven billion, up from one billion just two hundred years ago. The world escaped the "Malthusian trap" of population growth leading to mass starvation through economic productivity that was made possible by the emergent institutions of capital ownership, investment, and trade. If those institutions were to be harmed, impeded, or abolished, how would the capacity of the world's economy to feed, clothe, and heal a population of seven billion be affected? Indeed, would the world ever have supported the seven billion people who are alive today? These are sobering questions.

"Blessed Are the Poor" and "Woe unto You That Are Rich"

The rise of wealth and its distribution ever more widely among all classes of society also raises crucial questions of theology and biblical interpretation. When we read Jesus' words in the Beatitudes, "But woe unto you that are rich!" do we see them as articulating a political philosophy or policy? No doubt the Christian message has social and political implications. They are not the ultimate goal of the gospel, however, but rather effects flowing from the radical conversion of the heart of the person. The proper function of the government is not the redistribution of wealth but the adjudication of justice and the promotion of the common good, which is, "the sum total of social conditions which allow people...to reach their fulfillment...."[8] A just legal system will militate against the unjust acquisition and accumulation of wealth, whether on the part of governments—as when they plunder property in wars or through unjust taxation or inflationary monetary policy—or by thieves in back alleys.

The Jewish-Christian belief system is rooted in history. Both Judaism and Christianity are historical religions that derive much of their self-understanding from historical events—the Exodus and the Resurrection, for example—that were formative of their beliefs. Over time, the significance of those beliefs has come to be understood at a more profound level, with the development and refinement of their implications.

The writers of the biblical period lived in a pre-industrial agrarian economy, and the Bible contains true, but largely prescientific, conceptions and categories on the subject of economics. In a world informed by the experience of the Industrial Revolution and—even more recently—by the advance of communications technology and artificial intelligence, with more and more people throughout the world becoming more prosperous and living longer and better than their ancestors, it becomes imperative for the ongoing credibility of Christianity that Christian thinkers develop a clear understanding of matters pertaining to economics.

It is imperative that these realities of human existence be considered in the light of the whole of the Christian revelation, so that the gospel can be announced to new generations in an idiom that they can understand. In the decades ahead, as whole societies around the globe enter the circles of exchange and come to understand for themselves that markets produce prosperity, the new prosperity will present a real pastoral challenge to Christianity. To the extent that people understand the benefits and functioning of market economies, even if only on a practical level, institutions that fail to take into account these realities will lose their credibility as bearers of truth.

In order for the Church to be capable of confronting the moral challenges emerging in a world in which people are wealthier than ever before, it will need to recognize the inadequacy of holding up a subsistence-level agriculture-based economy—or redistributive policies that could return the world to such poverty—as the key to human flourishing. While it is certainly true that "ye have the poor with you always" (Mark 14:7), it is also true that the world population today has become enormously wealthier than even the wealthiest of those who first heard those words of Jesus.

Before the advent of modern capitalism and the Industrial Revolution, the rich were in great part state officials, tax collectors, court intellectuals, complicit clerics, merchants, and landowners benefiting from the monarch's favors, along with hangers-on who made a killing by trading access to such favors. The livelihoods of this tiny minority of lucky favored rich people depended largely on taxes, war, and plunder. But now wealth can be accumulated in productive activities that benefit society at large—and all but a tiny number of Americans, Western Europeans, and increasing numbers of Latins and Asians, as well as Africans, today, would qualify as "the rich" by biblical standards. The Western culture that formed around the Jewish-Christian ethic on work, on property, and against theft, meant that the whole world has become vastly more productive—and wealthier—than it was two thousand years ago.

As things continue to improve globally, it is critical for religious leaders in particular to address a moral question posed by that improvement.

Simply put, in the reality of human betterment as it has been unfolding over roughly the last century and a half, not everyone's life has improved or will improve at the same rate. Not every region or country will improve at the same time, or at the same speed. This lag easily invites envy, which can be turned to political use—in the name of a moral cause. But a sober and clear-minded grasp of what is actually happening on the economic plane may enable us to understand the choice for what it really is. When we look at how the world's population actually rose out of poverty, it becomes clear that redistribution of wealth is not the best path forward; on the contrary, creating broadly distributed wealth is the peaceful and viable path. That is the main economic lesson of the last few hundred years.

Is Jesus' injunction "woe unto you that are rich" a condemnation of wealth as such, or a warning against seeking wealth *as an end in itself*? As we have seen, Saint Paul doesn't say that money itself is evil, but rather that "the love of money is the root of all evil: which while some coveted after, they have erred from the faith, and pierced themselves through with many sorrows" (1 Timothy 6:10). It seems clear that this text is less about coins or dollars (or denarii or talents), or even about the making and accumulation of money, as it is about making the pursuit of material gain the purpose of one's life, independent of moral concerns. Ecclesiastes rounds out the picture by telling us, "He that loveth silver shall not be satisfied with silver; nor he that loveth abundance with increase: this is also vanity" (5:10).

Must We Sell All We Have?

Each of the synoptic Gospels preserves the memory of an occasion when a rich young man (or "ruler") approaches Jesus for spiritual direction (Matthew 19:16–21; Mark 10:17–29; Luke 18:18–30). The potential disciple apparently has a deep desire to live righteously. He asks, "Good Master, what shall I do that I may inherit eternal life?" (Mark 10:17). After reminding the young man of the commandments and being reassured that he has kept them all his life, Jesus seems to read this man's heart. He calls him to something even deeper than all his previous success and wealth: "Then Jesus beholding him loved him, and said unto him, One thing thou lackest: go thy way, sell whatsoever thou hast, and give to the poor, and thou shalt have treasure in heaven." He then gives the same invitation to him that he offered to Peter and Andrew: "Follow me" (Mark 10:21). I have joked that, had the man responded affirmatively, we might have had a thirteenth apostle.

This encounter sets the stage for Jesus' teaching on the radical nature and cost of discipleship. Here is where the famous phrase so often recounted in discussions about wealth and economic success arises: "how hard is it for them that trust in riches to enter into the kingdom of God! It is easier for a camel to go through the eye of a needle, than for a rich man to enter into the kingdom of God" (Mark 10:24–25). That vivid metaphor, which comes mid-way through the account, is perhaps its most memorable part.

Jesus' words are often seen as a denunciation of wealth, or an indication that wealth is incompatible with discipleship. Oddly, people rarely remember the entirety of Jesus' instruction.

In fact, the young man is first told that he should engage in commerce! Jesus says, "[G]o thy way, *sell* whatsoever thou hast, and give to the poor" [emphasis added]. The rich young man is not told to destroy his possessions or to simply *give away* all he has. Yet that is how most people remember this passage. That will come, to be sure, but *first* he is to sell all his possessions; to liquidate his ownings. To "liquidate" one's property is to make it more fluid (as the word suggests), that is, useable in a way it was not previously. When one sells something, one engages in an exchange of values. If this man hopes to maximally help the poor to whom the proceeds of the sale will eventually be given, presumably he will seek to get a good price for his estate. The eventual benefit to those in need would be the result of his profit-making abilities, and this very act of enterprise or exchange would become the way in which he would prove himself faithful to the command of Jesus. His wealth would be a tool—one that cannot be intrinsically evil, because Jesus commanded him to use it. And the same thing is true not only about his wealth, but about his engagement in commercial exchange: the profit that he would realize from the sale would become the means to benefit others.[9]

Of course, none of this ever transpired. The man gave up and went away sad "for he had great possessions" (Mark 10:22). Jesus sums up the encounter with a sober warning on the cost of discipleship: "Children, how hard is it for them that trust in riches to enter into the kingdom of God!" (Mark 10:24). Discipleship is indeed arduous, if taken seriously, because it will always require a sacrifice, a cross to be borne. And the crosses come in different shapes and sizes, depending on what is most important to each person. Now comes one of the most memorable metaphors in the whole of the Bible: "It is easier for a camel to go through the eye of a needle, than for a rich man to enter into the kingdom of God" (Mark 10:24). You can imagine how often I am asked about this verse. The final line of this pericope, on the other hand—the one that provides the key to understanding the whole encounter—is almost never remembered. Pause now for a moment without reading further, and see if you recall what it is: What does Jesus tell us is the moral of this story?

Jesus' own disciples are baffled: "And they were astonished out of measure, saying among themselves, Who then can be saved?" (Mark 10:26).

Now comes the gravamen. "With men it is impossible, but not with God: for with God all things are possible" (Mark 10:27).

Humanity, with all its abilities and achievements, cannot purchase an eternal relationship with God. The rich young man (and through him, each of us) is being taught a critical lesson: wealth cannot be the goal of our life. We must not "trust in riches." The young man was called to employ his talents—that is, to engage in commerce—but with a higher goal than the bottom line. He, and we, are to see wealth not as an end but as a means to a greater end—discipleship. How can this passage be interpreted to say that commerce or the wealth that it produces, is somehow intrinsically evil when Jesus clearly commands it?

The bigger picture came to me in seminary, on my first day in a course on moral theology, which I can still vividly recall. The professor began the class with a thought-provoking question: "Do you believe that the study of morality stands to make you a more moral person?"

A debate ensued, pro and con. In the end I concluded that the study of moral theology stood the chance of being dangerous—to the extent that I gained a greater awareness of my moral responsibilities, my obligation to live the moral law was likewise increased. While invincible ignorance may get us a pass, knowledge increases obligation. So does wealth.

And yet you can read a theologian arguing in a leading "conservative" journal that "the New Testament treats such [enormous] wealth not merely as a spiritual danger, and not merely as a blessing that should not be misused, but as *an intrinsic evil*" [emphasis added].[10] You would think that theologians, Bible scholars, and clergy would know better. But this misunderstanding is all too common.

A real understanding of what wealth is might clear the fog a bit, even if the challenge of how faithful believers ought to use abundant resources would remain. Isn't wealth simply the total resources or opportunities that people have at their disposal? As these resources and opportunities increase, so does the concomitant responsibility that these opportunities be used well, morally, and responsibly. We see this ethic expressed in the Gospels, for example in Luke 12:48, where we read, "For unto whomsoever much is given, of him shall be much required."

Against this backdrop, we can examine some of the other references related to our topic that can be found elsewhere in the New Testament.

You Cannot Serve God and Mammon

The word *mammon* is used in Matthew 6:24 and Luke 16:9–13. With a little bit of study, we learn that mammon derives from the Hebrew for "that in which one trusts" and that in Aramaic it means riches or wealth.[11] "Mammon" as it is used in the Bible, however, is not physical but spiritual: it refers to a frame of mind—distorted love, exaggerated affection, or imbalanced attachment to money. It is clear that Jesus qualifies his use of the term mammon, seeing it as sinful to the extent that money is served in preference to God. Thus while in both passages he says, "Ye cannot serve God and mammon" (Matthew 6:24, Luke 16:13), in Luke he speaks specifically of "the mammon of unrighteousness" and "the unrighteous mammon" (Luke 16:9). The condemnations and warnings about money or wealth in the New Testament entail concerns for the person's attitudes toward money—not simply its possession, much less the existence of it as such. As we saw in the story of the rich young man, it is not just "the rich" but specifically those who "trust in riches" that find it hard to enter the Kingdom.

Riches and Extravagance

One example of this balanced approach can be seen in Jesus' repeated references to the "rich." By asking ourselves what it meant to be rich in the world and time that Jesus spoke (first-century Palestine), we can gain a deeper insight into Jesus' message and intention. In a pre-industrial world, wealth and poverty were associated with things other than economics. Across the span of human history, wealth was largely static—and most frequently obtained by political manipulation, theft, and war. It was less frequently derived from trade, investment, or productivity, as we understand these concepts today.

For the most part, people living in economically free societies become wealthy not by expropriation or impoverishing others but precisely by cooperating with others, understanding the needs people have, and working to meet those needs. This requires bearing the risk inherent in all economic projects, employing greater efficiency in service by engaging others with respect, establishing a record of honesty and reliability, looking forward, being willing to delay immediate gratification for a future reward for your creativity. This is productivity. The prayer to God to "establish thou the work of our hands" in Psalm 90:17 is an apt example of a person's asking God that his activities, including financial ones, might be productive, successful, and even profitable.

Christianity hardly condemns this approach. On the contrary, if it did not exactly invent this way of creating wealth, Christianity brought form and substance and moral clarity to it. These are the values taught in Scripture, and this is the culture that would emerge from the words of the apostles and Jesus, and would be embodied by the saints and martyrs and lived by the finest and most noble political leaders and statesmen throughout history. The values of the gospel promote the common good, and when a whole society is shaped by those values over time, the benefits of virtuous behavior and the prosperity it creates can flow to all classes of the society. Some particularly creative, honest, risk-taking, industrious, and (yes) lucky people will be richer than others, but their extraordinary efforts will also benefit others, raising the general level of wealth and prosperity around them.

An opposite view can be seen in a book by José Porfirio Miranda. In *Communism in the Bible*, he writes that "no one can take the Bible seriously without concluding that according to it, the rich, for being rich, should be punished." He goes on to say, "All differentiating wealth is ill-gotten...therefore to be rich is to be unjust." [12]

But the fact is, many of the wealthy among us—brilliant and productive entrepreneurs, capitalists, investors—have participated in the creation of the world as we know it, with many benefits for those who are not accounted rich. In our world, as we have seen, wide-spread prosperity now supports an unprecedented population of seven billion people for the first time in history. In our world, the number of people living in poverty has been cut in half starting with the Industrial Revolution and going into the twentieth century—and then cut in half again in the twentieth century—as the talents and risks and hard work of inventors, entrepreneurs, and investors have been exercised in service to their fellow man in the market economy. For this "the rich" deserve our respect and praise, not a snide dismissal.

It is true that material success carries with it temptations to over-indulgence and to the use of one's wealth for purposes of power and not mere persuasion. Just so, poverty and want tempt many toward envy, bitterness, despair, and acts of theft. But in either case, the temptation can be resisted. Let's grant that we can distinguish the size of our bank accounts (whether high or low) from the status of our souls.

Our Lord's admonitions about riches should be mediated through the conscience of the believer, not the agency of the state. A more balanced approach will prevent us from adding legitimacy to the ambitions of the central state. We should take our cue from the way

Gregory the Great interpreted the story of the Rich Man and Lazarus: "For it was not poverty that led Lazarus to heaven, but humility; nor was it wealth that prevented the rich man from attaining eternal rest but rather his egoism and his infidelity."[13]

An ethical perspective on the possession of riches is well expressed in the Thirty-Ninth Psalm, which does not denounce wealth as such, but situates it in the broader context of human reality, and indeed, of eternity: "Behold, thou hast made my days as an handbreadth; and mine age is as nothing before thee: verily every man at his best state is altogether vanity. Surely every man walketh in a vain shew: surely they are disquieted in vain: he heapeth up riches, and knoweth not who shall gather them" (Psalm 39:5–6). This sobering and honest reflection, demonstrating how to hold wealth lightly in life is an example that can help us to cut through the tendency to hoard and clutch at riches. After all, even the greatest estate is minute when seen against the backdrop of eternity. This point, often forgotten by the very ones in a position to know it best, is a powerful corrective to the tendency to cling and hoard.

The Beatitudes, and Jesus' Wealthy Friends

The Beatitudes are among the most poetic and memorable sayings of Jesus recorded in the New Testament. But they are often made use of by those who want to turn the gospel into a political program. The Beatitudes are turned into political planks, deployed to decry economic productivity or wealth accumulation as greed. This can be accomplished only by taking the Lord's words too simplistically and selectively. That becomes clear if you simply read the Beatitudes in their context.

"Blessed be ye poor," says Jesus, "But woe unto you that are rich! for ye have received your consolation. Woe unto you that are full! for ye shall hunger. Woe unto you that laugh now! for ye shall mourn and weep." Surely these sentences do not constitute a denunciation of full stomachs or the experience of joy and laughter. We understand almost intuitively that in these references the lesson is about excess, not simply about conviviality or having enough to eat. To politicize these words, as some exegetes attempt to do, turning them into a call to redistribute wealth, does injustice to their original intention. Reducing the words of Jesus to a political platform makes a mockery of the profound point of the Lord's eloquent and challenging sermon—namely, that neither satisfaction nor heaven is attained by wealth, or any earthly pleasure or accomplishment.

A balanced exegesis requires us to employ the whole of Scripture, read against the backdrop of how Christians have read it throughout the ages and a historical understanding of what formed the Christian conscience for two thousand years. ("The lives of the saints are the footnotes to the Gospels," someone once said.)

While it is certainly the case that one of the distinctive characteristics of Jesus' ministry was his constant focus on the marginalized and outcasts, it would be far too materialistic to assume that this was only the economically marginal—though, of course, it certainly included them.

The clearest indication that Jesus reached out to marginalized classes beyond the poor is that his "table fellowship" was inclusive of broad classes of people.[14] There is a general agreement that this included the poor, but the poor in a broader sense than those lacking financial resources. The scribes and Pharisees remarked that Jesus ate with sinners and tax collectors—that is, with Jewish agents of the occupying Roman force, who were wealthy but were hated by other Jews.[15] Jesus also consorted with Samaritans, despite the fact, as Saint John's Gospel comments, "the Jews have no dealings with the Samaritans" (John 4:9). He also included women in his circle, particularly women who were outcast because they were known to be sinners, or who were caught in other difficult circumstances (whether moral or spiritual or physical). He helped Gentiles (see Matthew 8:5–13 and Luke 7:1–10), allowed lepers to get close to him (Matthew 8:2–3, Mark 1:40–42, and Luke 5:12–13), and famously said, " Suffer little children, and forbid them not, to come unto me: for of such is the kingdom of heaven" (Matthew 19:14). And while the Lord had conflicts with the religious leadership, some of even that class were his close disciples—Joseph of Arimathea, for example, was a member of the Sanhedrin (see Luke 15:43 and 23:50–51).

Jesus' conflicts with the rich were due more to their arrogance and pride than to their wealth; he condemned them for their disdain or disregard for the poor, rather than for their holdings. This becomes apparent in a number of the relationships Jesus shared with persons of means. More than any other woman besides Mary the mother of Jesus, Mary from Magdala (a village on the shore of the Sea of Galilee) is a central character in the Gospels. She accompanied Christ to the cross and was among the first to encounter the newly resurrected Lord. Jesus would entrust her with the mission to bring the news of his resurrection to his apostles, who were hiding out in Jerusalem. That fact has earned her the title of "Apostle to the Apostles." Over time, various confusions about Mary Magdalene in the Gospels have emerged owing to the lack of detailed information provided about her, as well as to the commonality of the name Mary among those close to Jesus: his mother, the sister of Martha and Lazarus, the wife of Clopas, and so forth. There is no evidence that Mary Magdalene was a reformed prostitute; what we know about Mary of Magdala is that she was a woman from whom seven devils had been exorcized (see Luke 8:2). Intriguing—and important for our purposes—is the question of her economic status.

In fact, Mary is described as one of a number of women who "ministered unto him of their substance" (Luke 8:3)—early benefactresses supporting the work of Jesus and his apostles. There were obviously some superfluous resources—the very definition of wealth—available to her and the other women mentioned. (During the Roman occupation, Magdala was considered one of the most prosperous cities, yielding extensive tax revenues. Perhaps this prosperity was linked to the Phoenician shell-dye factory which was excavated in the ruins of Magdala in 2019. Purple dye was rare in the ancient world and associated with the royalty who could afford its purchase.)

Jesus' example of enlisting and accepting the aid of wealthy benefactors was followed by Saint Paul in his encounter with Lydia, evidently a successful businesswoman in Thyatira, who may have derived her wealth from a similar enterprise as Mary Magdalene. Lydia, thought to be the first female Christian convert in Europe, hosted Saint Paul and his entire entourage at her home while he was on his mission (Acts 16:40–17:1).

Joseph of Arimathea, the follower of Jesus who, as we have seen, was a member of the Jewish religious leadership, is mentioned in all four Gospels. Matthew describes him as "a rich man" (Matthew 27:57), and all four Gospels report that he provided a tomb and a linen shroud for Jesus' burial (Matthew 27:57–61, Mark 15:43–47, Luke 23:50–55, and John 19:38–42).

Let us consider for a moment these intriguing references to the wrapping of Jesus' body in a linen cloth. This incident evokes the memory of the quaternion of Roman soldiers who, stripping Jesus at the crucifixion, discovered among the Lord's few possessions a garment "without seam, woven from the top throughout" that they deemed to be highly valuable (see John 19:23). This seamless garment might be likened to a Saville Row suit today, prompting us to ask how it is that an itinerant Jewish preacher who had "hath not where to lay his head" (Matthew 8:20), came into the possession of such an expensive article of clothing, and why, if he were viscerally disdainful of all the trappings of wealth as such, he had not discarded or given it away prior to Calvary?

The seamless garment, the rich man's tomb, the linen shroud, and—as we shall see—the anointing with expensive oil that Judas considered wasteful indicate that in addition to the poor and marginalized whom Jesus loved and was close to, there were also wealthy backers, both male and female, of his ministry who were also his close associates, and that Jesus did not condemn wealth in itself.

The Anointing of Jesus with Oil

Consider for a moment the extravagant anointing of Jesus' feet with "ointment of spikenard, very costly" (John 12:3). There are several renditions of Jesus' being anointed in different Gospels, with various details.

The accounts in Matthew (26:6–13) and Mark (14:3–9) both depict an unnamed woman, and neither mentions an exact cost for the oil. Luke (7:36–50) mentions a "sinful woman." As is often the case with the synoptic Gospels, these accounts are quite similar, each locating the place as the home of Simon, but differing in small details. John is the only Gospel writer to name the woman as Mary sister of Martha; he locates the event at their home in Bethany. Here is John's account:

> Then Jesus six days before the passover came to Bethany, where Lazarus was, which had been dead, whom he raised from the dead. There they made him a supper; and Martha served: but Lazarus was one of them that sat at the table with him. Then took Mary a pound of ointment of spikenard, very costly, and anointed the feet of Jesus, and wiped his feet with her hair: and the house was filled with the

odour of the ointment. Then saith one of his disciples, Judas Iscariot, Simon's son, which should betray him, Why was not this ointment sold for three hundred pence, and given to the poor? This he said, not that he cared for the poor; but because he was a thief, and had the bag, and bare what was put therein. Then said Jesus, Let her alone: against the day of my burying hath she kept this. For the poor always ye have with you; but me ye have not always. (John 12:1–8)

As our study focuses on the economic dimensions of the Gospels, I will leave aside the differences among the different Gospel accounts (and questions such as whether they are memories of two different events, or the same one), and concentrate on the essential line of the story and the economic questions that arise from it.

This act would represent an exceeding extravagance for a woman: perhaps her entire life's savings. The cost of the oil would have represented about a year's wage for a laborer. Let's look at the reaction to the lavishness of her display from those surrounding Jesus and this woman—whether from Judas, as named in John, or from unnamed disciples of Jesus, as in Matthew (26:8–9) and Mark (14:4–5)—and ask what we can learn from their response.

Consider the objection of Judas, as recounted by John: "Then saith one of his disciples, Judas Iscariot, Simon's son, which should betray him, Why was not this ointment sold for three hundred pence, and given to the poor?" (John 12:4–5). Judas' complaint voices the perennial juxtaposition of luxury with the needs of the poor—in economic terms, the zero-sum fallacy. This complaint about the anointing portrays things from a very common but rather truncated perspective. Judas sees only the cost of the nard, not the love that prompted the lavishness. As Jesus says, "Let her alone: against the day of my burying hath she kept this. For the poor always ye have with you; but me ye have not always" (John 12:7–8).

And, at least in the case of Judas, pretended concern for the poor is a cover for his own greed and dishonesty. Judas was actually speaking out of avarice—his desire to control the money that Mary had spent on the aromatic nard to anoint Jesus' feet: "This he said, not that he cared for the poor; but because he was a thief, and had the bag, and bare what was put therein" (John 12:6). His greed, which is the real motive for his pretended concern for the poor, blinds him to Mary's demonstrative love.

Even if it is genuine, a professed love for the poor is insufficient to actually improve their lives. It is all too easy to rail against the consumption of luxury goods and contrast that consumption with the dire conditions of the poor—without doing anything to realistically assist them.

The words of Jesus to Judas, "For the poor always ye have with you" (John 12:8) ought not to be seen as a dismissal of the tragedy of poverty, much less a discouragement of or disregard for the obligation to assist the poor—especially given the context, which is the assumed practice of charitable donations by Jesus and his disciples (see John 12:6 and 13:29). His words are, rather, an echo of Deuteronomy 15:11, which takes the fact that "the poor shall never cease" as a reason *for* showering charity on them: "For the poor shall never cease out of the land: therefore I command thee, saying, Thou shalt open thine hand wide unto thy brother, to thy poor, and to thy needy, in thy land."

The Cleansing of the Temple

The "cleansing of the Temple," as the account of Jesus throwing out the money changers is usually called, is easy fodder for those who want to claim that Jesus disdained economic exchange and commerce to promote the idea of a natural antagonism between money and God. But this superficial reading can only be maintained to the extent that a person is unwilling to probe the depths of the story and ask what Jesus actually intended by his actions.

The cleansing of the Temple is recounted in all four Gospels (Matthew 21:12–17, Mark 11:15–19, Luke 19:45–48, and at John 2:13–16), though again details among them differ. In Matthew's description, "And Jesus went into the temple of God, and cast out all them that sold and bought in the temple, and overthrew the tables of the moneychangers, and the seats of them that sold doves, and said unto them, It is written, My house shall be called the house of prayer; but ye have made it a den of thieves" (Matthew 21:12–13).

The cleansing of the Temple is the singular instance of Jesus' being associated with violence—something that is outside our purview, but notable in itself. As a result, much of the commentary on the incident is a running debate between just war theory and pacifism in Christian thought. Our attention is focused on what the action of Christ means as it relates to commercial activity and money—both its economic meaning and its theological meaning.

Pope Benedict XVI (Joseph Ratzinger) succinctly outlines a long-standing political interpretation of the ministry of Jesus in general, which portrays the confrontation in the Temple as a zealous act of violence against the Temple authorities, who were seen as collaborating with the Roman imperialist colonizers. As he points out, this line of commentary on the incident came to a crescendo in the 1960s. Ratzinger contrasts the political approach with an eschatological interpretation that portrays the cleansing of the Temple as an echo of Old Testament expectations.[16]

For some, the very expression "moneychangers" may connote greed, exploitation, and injustice. And the phrase "den of thieves" may lend credence to an interpretation that equates business with theft. But it is actually derived from Jeremiah 7:11: "Is this house, which is called by my name, become a den of robbers in your eyes? Behold, even I have seen it, saith the Lord." The phrase "den of robbers" sums up a list of iniquities such as murder, adultery, idolatry, false witness; "Behold, ye trust in lying words, that cannot profit. Will ye steal, murder, and commit adultery, and swear falsely, and burn incense unto Baal, and walk after other gods whom ye know not; and come and stand before me in this house, which is called by my name, and say, We are delivered to do all these abominations?" (Jeremiah 7:8–10).

Binding the Strong Man, by Ched Myers, is one example of a highly politicized, indeed revolutionary interpretation of this episode (and, for that matter, of the whole Gospel of Mark).[17] While conceding that Jesus was not surprised "as such" that there was commercial activity in the Temple, Myers concludes that, "It is the *ruling class interests* in control of the commercial enterprises in the temple market that Jesus is attacking" [emphasis in the original].[18] Myers sees Jesus' disruptive action as a call, "for an end to the entire cultic system … [which] represented the concrete mechanisms of oppression within a political economy that doubly exploited the poor and unclean."[19]

Rather than seeing Jesus' action as a response to a concrete injustice on the part of moneychangers who were cheating their fellow Jews by manipulating the currency, or recognizing the Lord's fundamentally eschatological intent, Myers contends that Jesus' intention was revolutionary: he meant to bring down the whole Temple and its entire "cultic system."

But in fact the moneychangers offered a necessary service to pilgrims, who would need to convert the currency they had arrived with, which often bore pagan imagery or the portrait of Caesar, who was worshipped by the Romans as a god (see Mark 12:15–17). Such imagery would be seen to defile the Temple; thus the need for an exchange of currency in the Court of the Gentiles. In addition, rather than having to find and purchase blemish-free animals suitable for sacrifice in the Temple at the local markets, pilgrims could obtain them more conveniently within the precincts of the Temple—also reducing the possibility of the sacrifices' being blemished in transport.[20]

But robbing pilgrims by overcharging them for the animals and by debasing the currency could also defile the Temple; in fact, such exploitation could be an even greater religious offense.[21] These violations of the Mosaic Law would be sufficient to enrage any worthy rabbi.

Rather than constituting reliable exegesis of the incident, the revolutionary political interpretations of this event betray an embedded hostility to commercial exchange as such, portraying all free exchange as a "den of thieves"—which is to say, a capitalist system of exploitation. But we must look elsewhere for the real cause of Jesus' ire. His attack on the moneychangers was not a rejection of the Temple (so central to Judaism) but a battle with the leadership—and a moment to point beyond them and even the Temple to ultimate realities.

Jesus' entire ministry, including his actions here, was directed to the higher goal of proclaiming the coming of the Kingdom of God, his ultimate mission. One notes, for example, in Matthew's account of the cleansing of the Temple, that the sick were brought to Jesus following his cleansing of the Temple—a juxtaposition that heightens the eschatological meaning of his actions, by anticipating the ultimate healing of the world with the coming of the eschaton. Note that the disruption of the money changers' tables brought to a halt not only whatever financial exploitation might have been occurring but the

Temple sacrifices themselves, which depended upon these exchanges—pointing to Christ's one supreme sacrifice for atonement.

We note, too, that in Matthew's account the cleansing of the Temple follows Jesus' royal and triumphal entry into Jerusalem. Taken together, these actions contain all sorts Messianic and kingly symbology. Compare Zechariah 14:21, Jeremiah 19:10, and 2 Kings 18:23. In the Hebrew Scriptures, dramatic gestures are often used to communicate a critical message.[22]

Despite the arguments of politically inclined interpreters culminating in the 1960s, Jesus' actions in the Temple were eschatological and not political in intent—pointing to a higher end (*telos*) and ultimate culmination, in Jesus' words, employed only in John, "my Father's house", a dwelling outside of time, to which all people are invited. It is a feast beyond limitations, where scarcity no longer pertains and where one can eat and drink at no cost, and not pay.[23]

"And the Spirit and the bride say, Come. And let him that heareth say, Come. And let him that is athirst come. And whosoever will, let him take the water of life freely" (Revelation 22:17). There are no costs in eternity, because there no scarcity of either time or resources there. Thus there is no economy as such in eternity.

Socialism in the Early Church?

Since at least the nineteenth century, if not even from the Middle Ages, there have been attempts to link Christianity to some kind of communist ideal. The classic comparison of the two in the nineteenth century is by Frederick Engels: "Both Christianity and the workers' socialism preach forthcoming salvation from bondage and misery; Christianity places this salvation in a life beyond, after death, in heaven; socialism places it in this world, in a transformation of society."[24]

Give Engels credit for at least drawing attention to a key difference between the two ways of thinking: one rejects utopia on earth while looking to eternity for salvation while the other wants salvation on earth while rejecting the idea of heaven. Engels thoroughly rejected the Christian perspective on salvation, preferring a utopian vision to be brought about by ideological, political, indeed violent means. Whether using totalitarian methods to bring heaven to earth is a wise undertaking is another question.

To this day there are thinkers anxious to erase the difference between eternity and time. They believe that Christianity itself should seek to bring about their vision of heaven in the here and now. A recent article penned for the *New York Times* by David Bentley Hart, a fellow at the Notre Dame Institute for Advanced Study and the author of *The New Testament: A Translation*," tended in this direction.[25] "It's true, of course, that the early church was not a political movement in the modern sense," he granted. Still, "the church *was* a kind of polity, and the form of life it assumed was not merely a practical strategy for survival, but rather the embodiment of its highest spiritual ideals. Its 'communism' was hardly incidental to the faith."

To what was Hart referring? See Acts 2:44–45 and 4:32–35: "And all that believed were together, and had all things common; And sold their possessions and goods, and parted them to all men, as every man had need.... And the multitude of them that believed were of one heart and of one soul: neither said any of them that ought of the things which he possessed was his own; but they had all things common. And with great power gave the apostles witness of the resurrection of the Lord Jesus: and great grace was upon them all. Neither was there any among them that lacked: for as many as were possessors of lands or houses sold them, and brought the prices of the things that were sold, and laid them down at the apostles' feet: and distribution was made unto every man according as he had need."

When you sit down and actually read the passages in the Acts of the Apostles, it is hard to believe that any honest exegete could derive socialism or a disregard for private property from their description of the solidarity of the early Christian Church. Reading these words, it seems remarkable that anyone can derive any form of ideological communism from this description.

To begin with, these were obviously extraordinary times. The early Christians were living in expectation of Jesus' imminent return and under constant threat from the authorities. Extraordinary circumstances justify extraordinary arrangements, which are not necessarily a model for ordinary times. Imagine yourself on a neighborhood block just hit by a hurricane. All roads in and out are blocked. Some people have food, and some do not. All the neighbors get together and help each other, knowing that at some point normalcy will return. There is no refrigeration so the meat will thaw regardless. People cook it up and share it with each other. People whose homes have been destroyed stay with those who still have shelter. Those with extra water share with those without. This sort of thing happens in communities all over the world in emergencies because people are good people and care for each other in times of need. The story of the early Christians sharing "all things [in] common" is a similarly inspirational story, part of the early history of a faith that would come to change the world.

Why must we politicize this event? Why take a model meant for extraordinary circumstances, call it communism, and then agitate for it to be imposed across the board by government? Imagine if one of the neighbors in the hurricane-hit neighborhood piped up at the end of the emergency and said: let's live this way forever! Most people would have better sense than to take that suggestion seriously.

These early Christian practices in times of great poverty and fear were voluntary acts inspired by the call of the gospel. They are a great illustration and witness of the inspiration Christianity provides to care for one's neighbor. Modern economies, though in a less dramatic way, instantiate these sentiments in charitable institutions, nonprofits, soup kitchens, and other kinds of philanthropy—all institutions inspired by the powerful truth that not all of people's material needs can be met through production and trade alone, that there are necessities that exceed what any market can provide. Perhaps this principle is most intimately and commonly exemplified by the family as an institution of giving and sharing, and by the *koinonia* that Christians share at the Lord's table.

To read these passages as social and political, rather than fundamentally sacramental and moral, is to distort the Gospel accounts by forcing them into an economistic and materialistic template. This is not exegesis but politics, not spirituality but ideology. To interpret these passages as somehow hostile to private property is to completely miss the difference between redistributing property and *sharing* it. This interpretation obscures the radical nature of the Christian claim about the Church as the Body of Christ, the communion of the saints who constitute "one bread, and one body: for we are all partakers of that one bread" (1 Corinthians 10:17).

Luke Timothy Johnson, a New Testament scholar with expertise on Luke and Acts, has written a deep dive into the way in which Saint Luke (the author of both books) treats possessions throughout his writings.[26] While Johnson's treatment of this subject is far too technical and expansive for the general readership for whom this book is intended, he does provide a key corrective to the interpretation I have outlined above. Johnson makes a commonsense but often overlooked critical observation that is applicable well beyond Luke, but particularly important for an accurate understanding of what "all things [in] common" meant for the first century church. To the extent that private property is diminished, so too is charity, which is fundamental to the Christian life. As Johnson points out, "A community of goods would make the giving of alms impossible."[27]

More broadly, Johnson shows that in Saint Luke's writings "poor" represents an outsider status more than an economic status—the "low estate" of Mary in the Magnificat (Luke 1:48), which indicates humility rather than just monetary poverty specifically.[28] Conversely, when we see Jesus go to the home of Zacchaeus, who "was rich," we remember that as a tax collector he too was an outcast—which is why the crowd "all murmured" when Jesus "received him joyfully" (Luke 19:6–7). Johnson shows that "poverty is not an economic designation, but a designation of spiritual status."[29]

To turn the description of Acts 2:44 of holding "all things [in] common" into a socialist paradigm that abolishes and prohibits private property is to turn the entire meaning of the first-century Christian experience on its head; it simply overlooks the fuller description of this same arrangement a few passages later in Acts 5:1–11, where the ownership and control of the property of Ananias and Sapphira is quite explicitly affirmed by no less an authority than Saint Peter himself who says, "While it remained unsold, did it not remain your own. And after it was sold, was it not at your disposal?" (verse 4).

Christianity as shown in the Book of Acts neither expropriated anyone's property nor forced them to "share" it. Instead, early Christianity *inspired* people to share—to surrender their own legitimate possessions out of love.

The call of the gospel transcends both the claims of civil law and all economic systems—at the same time as it is more radical in the demands it makes upon the conscience. It is a great error to confuse the two. In the order of grace, it may indeed be said that things are held in common: no one is turned away from the ministrations of the Christian church based on economic class.[30]

But Christians today are confused about wealth, private property, and our moral obligation to relieve the needs of the poor. The Scriptural morality of charity and generosity came to form an entire social ethic. But that morality is moored in the voluntary nature of the Christian commitment. And when Christians allow that morality to come lose from its moorings, it morphs into something altogether different. Christians then confuse interior and exterior forms of constraint—mistaking politics for morality.

It is the very absence of exterior obligation that makes Christianity so radical. How can we share something if we do not own it in the first place? So much of this confusion could be cleared up if we asked what it is that governs our moral life. Is it edicts of the state or the interior reign of Christ in the human heart?

The practical and life-affirming themes that we find in the parables are not outlier themes in the Gospels—they are the core of Jesus' message. They are illustrative of the broader principles of the Christian faith, and of the moral and spiritual urgency of living in a Christ-like way. They are a prescription for a well-lived life, not a political model to impose via public authority. The parables are illustrative stories, compelling and evocative vehicles to help us understand spiritual principles in a more practical way, in a manner that points to higher and more difficult-to-grasp truths.

What are the social implications? Our temple always needs cleansing, the rooting out of moral corruption. That is true of us as individuals, as a society, and as a political order. Until we dispense with our ideological biases and presuppositions, and gain clarity on precisely what those moral principles are that Jesus' parables teach, we risk destroying rather than cleansing.

Tearing up the fabric of functioning and vibrant markets is not a moral path; it threatens wreckage rather than purity. Our study of the parables points to the path forward. To reform society, we need wisdom, prudence, clarity of purpose, and a realistic understanding of the institutions we are reforming. The parables primarily focus on the practical moral problems that face all of us in our daily lives. They begin the cleansing process within us and often teach surprising lessons. The Gospels further elaborate with an inspired history of a salvific mission. We can still learn from these Scriptures today, provided we are humble enough to sit at the Master's feet and be taught.

Acknowledgements

Virtually no human endeavor is accomplished on a purely individual level, if for no other reason than that human beings are never themselves purely individual. We are in some kind of relationship from the first moment of our existence. And, so it is with this book.

Not to draw too august an analogy, but these chapters went through a process not unlike the Gospels themselves: the first level of reflection was drawn from homilies I had delivered over many years of pastoral work, some recorded on written manuscripts, more often in outlines and sketches. Numerous, varied, and scattered notes and scraps of whatever paper was at hand also helped me to recall an insight I found useful to communicate a new perspective or application. Long ago I picked up a habit from the model of (now Saint) Pope John Paul II who often prayed with a pen and note pad at hand, and many of these reflections, too, contain material found in redacted form in these pages.

Sharing some of these musings with trusted friends and colleagues helped me to fill gaps as they pointed out sources and ideas that would give more depth and substance to my thought, all of which came to be incorporated in this text.

I am particularly grateful to Jeff Tucker who early on aided me in this process by untangling my notes and untying many knots in the original transcripts and in offering keen economic connections. And to Professor Klyne Snodgrass, a major scholar of the parables, who took time from his own writing schedule to read this manuscript and enhance its content.

Likewise, my appreciation goes to my ever-dependable (and often opinionated) colleagues at the Acton Institute for all their indefatigable and inspirational work to advance the cause of the free and virtuous society. Among these especially is Kris Mauren, with whom I co-founded the Acton Institute in 1990 and who has succeeded me as its president. My faithful, ever-patient, and detailed assistant Katharine Harger, kept the ship on course. Nathan Mech was extremely helpful in an early reading of the draft. Dr. Sam Gregg, Dylan Pahman, and Dan Hugger also added helpful suggestions and helped me track down source material. From our small army of Acton interns who could be relied upon for a myriad of tasks, I wish to thank Isabella Maciejewski, Maggie Tynan, Maryn Setsuda, and Michaela Page for help in this regard. A businessman himself, my long-time friend David Milroy was a great encouragement in completing the book.

It is an honor once again to be associated with one of America's more venerable publishing houses, Regnery, which has fought the good fight for human freedom for three quarters of a century; and to work again with its *editor par excellence*, Elizabeth Kantor, who polished my pearls and "murdered some (but not too many) of my darlings." Thanks too, to their able copyeditor Laura Spence Swain.

Though this book came to fruition by the help of these many collaborators, the final redaction remains, of course, my own responsibility.

Selected Bibliography

Amplified Holy Bible. London: Zondervan, 2017.

Aquinas, Thomas. *Summa Theologiae*. London: Blackfriars, 1975.

Augustine of Hippo. *The Confessions*. Translated by F. J. Sheed. Indianapolis, Indiana: Hackett, 2006.

Babylonian Talmud, The (Seder Nezikin). *Baba Metzia*. Translated by H. Freedman. New York: Rebecca Bennet Publications Inc., 1959.

"Bankruptcy Law in the United States." Economic History Association. https://eh.net/encyclopedia/bankruptcy-law-in-the-united-states/.

Benedict, XVI, Pope. *Deus caritas est* (encyclical letter). The Vatican, 2005. http://www.vatican.va/content/benedict-xvi/en/encyclicals/documents/hf_ben-xvi_enc_20051225_deus-caritas-est.html.

Biblia Sacra: Juxta Vulgatam Clementinam. Edited by Michael Tweedale. London: Baronius Press, 2008.

Blomberg, Craig. "Jesus, Sinners, and Table Fellowship." *Bulletin for Biblical Research* 19, no. 1 (2009): 35–62.

"Brief History of Bankruptcy, A." Bankruptcy Data. https://www.bankruptcydata.com/a-history-of-bankruptcy.

Brown, Raymond et al. *The New Jerome Biblical Commentary*. Englewood, New Jersey: Prentice Hall, 1990.

Bruenig, Elizabeth. "How Augustine's Confessions and Left Politics Inspired My Conversion to Catholicism." *America Magazine,* July 25, 2017. https://www.americamagazine.org/faith/2017/07/25/how-augustines-confessions-and-left-politics-inspired-my-conversion-catholicism.

Çam, Deniz. "The Biggest Billionaire Winners and Losers of 2019." *Forbes,* December 20, 2019. https://www.forbes.com/sites/denizcam/2019/12/20/the-biggest-billionaire-winners-and-losers-of-2019/#4dc47bcc3ec2.

Cardenal, Ernesto. *The Gospel in Solentiname.* Maryknoll, New York: Orbis, 1972.

Catechism of the Catholic Church, The Vatican, 2309. http://www.vatican.va/archive/ENG0015/_P81.HTM.

Chafuen, Alejandro. *Faith and Liberty.* Lanham, Maryland: Lexington Books, 2003.

Churchill, Winston. "The Cause of the Left-Out Millions." Speech at Saint Andrew's Hall, Glasgow. In *Never Give In! The Best of Winston Churchill's Speeches,* selected and edited by his grandson Winston S. Churchill. London: Pimlico, 2004.

Cowan, David. *Economic Parables The Monetary Teachings of Jesus Christ.* London: Paternoster, 2006.

Dreier, Peter. "Jesus Was a Socialist." HuffPo. December 26, 2017. https://www.huffpost.com/entry/jesus-was-a-socialist_b_13854296.

Engels, Frederick. "On the History of Early Christianity." Marxists Internet Archive. https://www.marxists.org/archive/marx/works/1894/early-christianity/index.htm.

Fernandez, Francis. *In Conversation with God: Meditations for Each Day of the Year.* 2 vols. Strongsville, Ohio: Scepter Publishing, 1989.

Fitzmyer, Joseph. *The Gospel According to Luke*. 2 vols. New York: Doubleday, 1981–85.

Fonck, Leopold. *The Parables of Christ: An Exegetical and Practical Explanation*. Edited by George O'Neill. Fort Collins, Colorado: Roman Catholic Books, 1997.

Francis, Pope. *Fratelli tutti* (encyclical letter). The Vatican. October 3, 2020. http://www.vatican.va/content/francesco/en/encyclicals/documents/papa-francesco_20201003_enciclica-fratelli-tutti.html.

Fuglie, Keith O., James M. MacDonald, and Eldon Ball. *Productivity Growth in U.S. Agriculture* no. 9 (September 2007). https://www.ers.usda.gov/webdocs/publications/42924/11854_eb9_1_.pdf.

Gadenz, Pablo. *Catholic Commentary on Sacred Scripture: The Gospel of Luke*. Grand Rapids: Baker Academic, 2018.

Gregory the Great. *St. Gregory the Great: Homilies on the Gospel of St. Luke*, as cited in Fernandez, Francis, *In Conversation with God: Meditations for Each Day of the Year*. 2 vols. Strongsville, Ohio: Scepter Publishing, 1989.

Griswold, Daniel. *Mad about Trade: Why Main Street America Should Embrace Globalization*. Cato Institute, 2009.

Hart, David Bentley. "Are Christians Supposed to Be Communists?" *New York Times*, November 4, 2017. https://www.nytimes.com/2017/11/04/opinion/sunday/christianity-communism.html.

———. "Mammon Ascendent." *First Things*, June 2016.

Hayek, F. A. *The Fatal Conceit: The Errors of Socialism*. Edited by W. W. Bartley. Chicago: University of Chicago Press, 1988.

Holy Bible English Standard Version. Wheaton, Illinois: Crossway, 2018.

Holy Bible King James Version. Nashville, Tennessee: Thomas Nelson, 2021.

Holy Bible New King James Version. Nashville, Tennessee: Thomas Nelson, 1982.

Holy Bible Revised Standard Version. The Division of Christian Education of the National Council of the Churches of Christ in the United States of America, 1971.

Holy Bible Revised Standard Version Catholic Edition. Ignatius, 1994.

Hultgren, Arland J. *The Parables of Jesus: A Commentary.* Grand Rapids, Michigan: Wm. B. Eerdmans Pub. Co., 2000.

Jeremias, Joachim. *Jerusalem in the Time of Jesus.* Philadelphia: Fortress Press, 1969.

——. *The Parables of Jesus Second Revised Edition.* Hoboken, New Jersey: Prentice Hall, 1972.

——. *Rediscovering the Parables.* New York: Charles Scribner's Sons, 1968.

John Paul II. *Centesimus annus.* Encyclical Letter. The Vatican. May 1, 1991. http://www.vatican.va/content/john-paul-ii/en/encyclicals/documents/hf_jp-ii_enc_01051991_centesimus-annus.html.

Johnson, Luke T. *The Literary Function of Possessions in Luke–Acts.* Missoula, Montana: Scholars' Press, 1977.

Josephus, Flavius. *The Antiquities of the Jews.* Translated by William Whiston. Blacksburg, Virginia: William Whiston Unabridged Books, 2011.

——. *The Jewish War.* Translated by Martin Hammond. Oxford University Press, 2017.

Jowett, Benjamin. *The Dialogues of Plato in Five Volumes.* 3rd ed., vol. 3. Oxford, United Kingdom: Oxford University Press, 1892. https://www.john-uebersax.com/plato/myths/ship.htm

Kuttner, Robert. *Everything for Sale: The Virtues and Limits of Markets.* Chicago: University of Chicago Press, 1999.

Lapide, Cornelius Cornelii à. *The Great Commentary of Cornelius à Lapide: The Holy Gospel According to Luke.* Fitzwilliam, New Hampshire: Loreto Publications, 2008.

———. *The Great Commentary of Cornelius à Lapide.* vol. 2, book 9, chapter 35. Fitzwilliam, New Hampshire: Loreto Publications, 2008.

Levine, Amy-Jill. *Short Stories by Jesus: The Enigmatic Parables of a Controversial Rabbi.* New York: HarperOne, 2014.

Marx, Karl. *Capital: A Critique of Political Economy.* Edited by Frederick Engels. Translated from the 3rd German edition by Samuel Moore and Edward Aveling. Chicago: Charles H. Kerr & Company, 1909.

Mattera, Philip. "Debt Trap." Corporate Research Project. https://www.corp-research.org/e-letter/debt-trap.

McDowell, Erin. "These 10 Billionaires Have All Gone Broke or Declared Bankruptcy—Read the Wild Stories of How They Lost Their Fortunes." *Business Insider.* March 26, 2020. https://www.businessinsider.com/rich-billionaires-who-declared-bankruptcy-2019-7.

"Mediation." TWM Solicitors. https://www.twmsolicitors.com/our-services/dispute-resolution/wills-estate-administration-and-distribution-disputes/mediation/.

Meier, John P. A *Marginal Jew.* vol. 5. *Probing the Authenticity of the Parables.* New Haven, Connecticut: Yale University Press, 2016.

Miranda, José Porfirio. *Communism in the Bible.* Maryknoll, New York: Orbis, 1992.

von Mises, Ludwig. *Socialism: An Economic and Sociological Analysis.* London: Jonathan Cape, 1974.

Mitch, Curtis and Edward Sri. *Catholic Commentary on Sacred Scripture: The Gospel of Matthew.* Grand Rapids, Michigan: Baker Publishing.

Morse, Jennifer Roback. "The Modern State as an Occasion of Sin." *Heartland Policy Study* no. 71 (February 1, 1996). http://heartland.org/policy-documents/no-71-modern-state-occasion-sin.

Myers, Ched, *Binding the Strong Man: A Political Reading of Mark's Story of Jesus Twentieth Anniversary Edition*. Maryknoll, New York: Orbis Books, 2017.

Mueller, Jennifer. "How to Solve Inheritance Disputes with Mediation." Wikihow Legal. October 21, 2021. https://www.wikihow .legal/Solve-Inheritance-Disputes-with-Mediation.

Nolland, John. "The Role of Money and Possessions in the Parable of the Prodigal Son (Luke 18:11–32)." In Craig G. Bartholomew, Joel B. Green, and Anthony C. Thiselton, *Reading Luke: Interpretation, Reflection, Formation*, Scripture and Hermenetuics 7. Grand Rapids, Michigan: Zondervan, 2005.

Pfund, Colbey. "Five Reasons to Reinvest in Your Own Company." *Forbes*, October 2, 2018. https://www.forbes.com/sites/theyec/2018 /10/02/five-reasons-to-reinvest-in-your-own-company/ #60462da62da4.

Ratzinger, Joseph (Pope Benedict XVI). *Jesus of Nazareth: From the Baptism in the Jordan to the Transfiguration*. Translated by Adrian J. Walker. New York: Doubleday, 2007.

——. *Jesus of Nazareth: Holy Week*. San Francisco: Ignatius Press, 2011.

Roover, Raymond de. *Business, Banking, and Economic Thought in Late Medieval and Early Modern* Europe. Chicago: University of Chicago Press, 1975.

Schmalz, Matthew. "Taxing the Rich to Help the Poor? Here's What the Bible Says." The Conversation. December 10, 2017. https:// theconversation.com/taxing-the-rich-to-help-the-poor-heres -what-the-bible-says-88627.

Schumpeter, Joseph. *History of Economic Analysis*. Oxford, United Kingdom: Oxford University Press, 1996.

Scott, Bernard Brandon. *Hear Then the Parable: A Commentary on the Parables of Jesus*. Minneapolis, Minnesota: Fortress Press, 1990.

Second Vatican Council. *Gaudium et spes*. https://www.vatican.va/archive/hist_councils/ii_vatican_council/documents/vat-ii_const_19651207_gaudium-et-spes_en.html.

Seneca, Lucius Anneaus. *Seneca's Morals; by Way of Abstract: To Which Is Added, a Discourse under the Title of After-thought*. Translated by Roger L'Estrange. London: Sherwood, Neely and Jones, 1818.

Singer, Isidore, *The Jewish Encyclopedia: A Descriptive Record of the History, Religion, Literature, and Customs of the Jewish People from the Earliest Times to the Present Day*. New York: Funk and Wagnalls Company, 1905.

Snodgrass, Klyne. *Stories with Intent: A Comprehensive Guide to the Parables of Jesus*. Grand Rapids, Michigan: William B. Eerdmans, 2008.

——. "The Temple Incident" in *Key Events in the Life of the Historical Jesus: A Collaborative Exploration of Context and Coherence*. Edited by Darrell L. Bock and Robert L. Webb. Tübingen, Germany: Mohr Siebeck, 2009.

Taylor, Kyle. "Why You Need to Reinvest Half of What You Earn Back into Your Company." *Entrepreneur*, June 23, 2015. https://www.entrepreneur.com/article/247614.

Teresa of Calcutta. "Called to Profess, Not Success." Catholic Life, March 28, 2017. https://catholiclife.diolc.org/2017/03/28/called-to-profess-not-success/.

Tosato, Angelo. *Vangelo e Ricchezza: Nuove Prospettive Esegetiche; a cura di Dario Antiseri, Francesco D'Agostino e Angelo Petroni*. Rubbettion: Soveria Mannelli, 2002.

Varela, Adrián Francisco and Qayyah Moynihan. "17 Billionaires Who Lost the Most in the Past Year." *Business Insider*, January 23, 2019. https://www.businessinsider.com/the-17-billionaires-who -made-the-biggest-losses-in-the-past-year-2018-2019-1.

"What Is Inheritance Dispute Resolution?" Attorneys.com. http:// www.attorneys.com/wills-trusts-and-probate/trusts-and-estates /inheritance-dispute-resolution.

von Wieser, Friedrich. "Return Value." In *Natural Value*. Edited with a Preface and Analysis by William Smart. London: Macmillan, 1893. Book 3, Part 1, Chapter 1. https://oll-resources.s3.us-east -2.amazonaws.com/oll3/store/titles/1685/Wieser_1282_EBk_v6.o.pdf.

Notes

Introduction: The Enduring Power of the Parables

1. Pope Benedict XVI, *Jesus of Nazareth: From the Baptism in the Jordan to the Transfiguration*, trans. Adrian J. Walker (New York: Doubleday, 2007), 183.

2. Benjamin Jowett, *The Dialogues of Plato in Five Volumes*, 3rd ed., vol. 3 (Oxford: Oxford University, 1892), 184–89, https://www.john-uebersax.com/plato/myths/ship.htm.

3. Lucius Annaeus Seneca, *Seneca's Morals; by Way of Abstract: To Which Is Added, a Discourse under the Title of After-thought*, trans. Roger L'Estrange (London: Sherwood, Neely and Jones, 1818), 346. "And there may be great use made also of parables: for the way of application does usually more affect the mind, than the downright meaning."

4. Isidore Singer, *The Jewish Encyclopedia: A Descriptive Record of the History, Religion, Literature, and Customs of the Jewish People from the Earliest Times to the Present* Day (New York: Funk and Wagnalls Company, 1905), 71.

5. Except where otherwise noted, all Bible quotations in this book are from the King James Version.

6. Benedict XVI, *Jesus of Nazareth* (New York: Doubleday, 2007), 191–92.

7. Leopold Fonck, *The Parables of Christ: An Exegetical and Practical Explanation*, ed. George O'Neill (Fort Collins, Colorado: Roman Catholic Books, 1997).

8. Joachim Jeremias, *Rediscovering the Parables* (New York: Charles Scribner's Sons, 1968).

9. Bernard Brandon Scott, *Hear Then the Parable: A Commentary on the Parables of Jesus* (Minneapolis, Minnesota: Fortress Press, 1990).

10. Pope John Paul II, *Centesimus annus*, The Vatican, May 1, 1991, http://www.vatican.va/content/john-paul-ii/en/encyclicals/documents/hf_jp-ii_enc_01051991_centesimus-annus.html, sec. 32: "...the *role* of disciplined and

creative *human work* and, as an essential part of that work, *initiative and entrepreneurial ability* becomes increasingly evident and decisive.... This process, which throws practical light on a truth about the person which Christianity has constantly affirmed, should be viewed carefully and favourably."

Chapter 1: *The Hidden Treasure*

1. Leopold Fonck, *The Parables of Christ: An Exegetical and Practical Explanation*, ed. George O'Neill (Fort Collins, Colorado: Roman Catholic Books, 1997), 182.
2. New King James Version (Nashville, Tennessee: Thomas Nelson, 1982).

Chapter 2: *The Pearl of Great Price*

1. *Biblia Sacra: Juxta Vulgatam Clementinam*, ed. Michael Tweedale (London: Baronius Press, 2008), Novum Testamentum, 20.
2. Leopold Fonck, *The Parables of Christ: An Exegetical and Practical Explanation*, ed. George O'Neill (Fort Collins: Roman Catholic Books, 1997), 196.
3. Cornelius Cornelii à Lapide, *The Great Commentary of Cornelius à Lapide* vol. 2 (Fitzwilliam, New Hampshire: Loreto Publications, 2008), book 9, chapter 35.

Chapter 3: *The Sower*

1. Bernard Brandon Scott, *Hear Then the Parable* (Minneapolis, Minnesota: Fortress Press, 1990), 344.
2. Joachim Jeremias, *Rediscovering the Parables* (New York: Charles Scribner's Sons, 1968), 118.
3. Thomas Aquinas, *Summa Theologiae* (London: Blackfriars, 1975), II–II, q. 66, a. 2.
4. John Paul II, *Centesimus annus*, The Vatican, May 1, 1991, section 35, https://www.vatican.va/content/john-paul-ii/en/encyclicals/documents/hf_jp-ii_enc_01051991_centesimus-annus.html.
5. Pope Francis, *Fratelli tutti*, The Vatican, October 3, 2020, section 168, http://www.vatican.va/content/francesco/en/encyclicals/documents/papa-francesco_20201003_enciclica-fratelli-tutti.html; Robert Kuttner, *Everything for Sale: The Virtues and Limits of Markets* (Chicago: University of Chicago Press, 1999).

Chapter 4: *The Laborers in the Vineyard*

1. Bernard Brandon Scott, *Hear Then the Parable* (Minneapolis, Minnesota: Fortress Press, 1989), 291; Alejandro Chafuen cites the Late-Scholastic economist

Juan de Molina on a related theme in *Faith and Liberty* (Lanham, Maryland: Lexington Books, 2003), 106. "After considering the service that an individual undertakes and the large or small number of people who, at the same time, are found in similar service, if the wage that is set for him is at least the lowest wage that is customarily set in that region at that time for people in such service, the wage is to be considered just."

2. Friedrich von Wieser, "Return Value" in *Natural Value*, ed. William Smart (London: Macmillan, 1893), book 3, part 1, chapter 1, https://oll-resources.s3.us-east-2.amazonaws.com/oll3/store/titles/1685/Wieser_1282_EBk_v6.0.pdf.

3. Jennifer Roback Morse, "No. 71 The Modern State as an Occasion of Sin," The Heartland Institute, February 1, 1996, https://www.heartland.org/publications-resources/publications/no-71-the-modern-state-as-an-occasion-of-sin.

Chapter 5: *The Rich Fool*

1. Deuteronomy 21:17.

2. Elizabeth Bruenig, "How Augustine's Confessions and Left Politics Inspired My Conversion to Catholicism," *America*, July 25, 2017, https://www.americamagazine.org/faith/2017/07/25/how-augustines-confessions-and-left-politics-inspired-my-conversion-catholicism; Matthew Schmalz, "Taxing the Rich to Help the Poor? Here's What the Bible Says," The Conversation, December 10, 2017, https://theconversation.com/taxing-the-rich-to-help-the-poor-heres-what-the-bible-says-88627; Peter Dreier, "Jesus Was a Socialist," HuffPo, December 26, 2017, https://www.huffpost.com/entry/jesus-was-a-socialist_b_13854296.

3. Winston Churchill, "The Cause of the Left-Out Millions" (October 11, 1906, Saint Andrew's Hall, Glasgow) in *Never Give In! The Best of Winston Churchill's Speeches*, ed. Winston S. Churchill (London: Pimlico, 2004), 23.

4. See, for example, "What Is Inheritance Dispute Resolution?," Attorneys.com, http://www.attorneys.com/wills-trusts-and-probate/trusts-and-estates/inheritance-dispute-resolution; "Mediation," TWM Solicitors, https://www.twmsolicitors.com/our-services/dispute-resolution/wills-estate-administration-and-distribution-disputes/mediation/; Jennifer Mueller, "How to Solve Inheritance Disputes with Mediation," Wikihow Legal, October 21, 2021, https://www.wikihow.legal/Solve-Inheritance-Disputes-with-Mediation.

5. Cornelius Cornelii à Lapide, *The Great Commentary of Cornelius à Lapide: The Holy Gospel According to Luke* (Fitzwilliam, New Hampshire: Loreto Publications, 2008), 486.

6. Arland J. Hultgren, *The Parables of Jesus: A Commentary* (Grand Rapids: William B. Eerdmans Pub. Co., 2000), 107.

7. Ibid., 108.

8. Kyle Taylor, "Why You Need to Reinvest Half of What You Earn Back into Your Company," *Entrepreneur*, June 23, 2015, https://www.entrepreneur.com/article/247614; Colbey Pfund, "Five Reasons to Reinvest in Your Own Company," *Forbes*, October 2, 2018, https://www.forbes.com/sites/theyec/2018/10/02/five-reasons-to-reinvest-in-your-own-company/#60462da62da4.

Chapter 6: The Two Debtors

1. Joachim Jeremias, *Rediscovering the Parables* (New York: Charles Scribner's Sons, 1968), 99.

2. Karl Marx, *Capital: A Critique of Political Economy*, translated from the 3rd German edition by Samuel Moore and Edward Aveling, ed. Frederick Engels (Chicago: Charles H. Kerr & Company, 1909).

3. Exodus 22:25–27; Leviticus 25:36–37; Deuteronomy 23:20–21.

4. See "Bankruptcy Law in the United States," Economic History Association, https://eh.net/encyclopedia/bankruptcy-law-in-the-united-states/; "A Brief History of Bankruptcy," Bankruptcy Data, https://www.bankruptcydata.com/a-history-of-bankruptcy; Philip Mattera, "Debt Trap," Corporate Research Project, https://www.corp-research.org/e-letter/debt-trap.

5. Leopold Fonck, *The Parables of Christ: An Exegetical and Practical Explanation*, ed. George O'Neill (Fort Collins, Colorado: Roman Catholic Books, 1997), 678.

Chapter 7: The Talents

1. This phrase of Jesus (English Standard Version, Matthew 25:15; the King James Version reads "to every man according to his several ability") has been lifted and politicized by Marx and his followers for their own rather different purposes. See, for example, https://halshs.archives-ouvertes.fr/halshs-01973833/document.

2. Flavius Josephus, *The Jewish War*, trans. Martin Hammond (Oxford: Oxford University Press, 2017), book 2, chapter 4, verse 2.

3. Bernard Brandon Scott, *Hear Then the Parable: A Commentary on the Parables of Jesus* (Minneapolis, Minnesota: Fortress Press, 1990), 220.

4. Arland J. Hultgren, *The Parables of Jesus: A Commentary* (Grand Rapids, Michigan: Wm. B. Eerdmans Pub. Co., 2000), 274.

5. Ibid., 8.

6. *The Babylonian Talmud* (Seder Nezikin), *Baba Metzia* vol. 1, trans. H. Freedman (New York: Rebecca Bennet Publications Inc., 1959), 250–51.

7. It is interesting to compare the attitude of this failed servant to his master with Karl Marx's attitude toward entrepreneurship: "Accumulation of wealth at one pole is, therefore, at the same time accumulation of misery, agony of toil slavery, ignorance, brutality, mental degradation, at the opposite pole, *i.e.,* on the side of the class that produces its own product in the form of capital." Karl Marx, *Capital*, vol. 1, ch. 25, https://www.marxists.org/archive/marx/works/1867-c1/ch25.htm; "Capitalist production, therefore, develops technology, and the combining together of various processes into a social whole, only by sapping the original sources of all wealth-the soil and the labourer." Karl Marx, *Capital*, vol. 1, ch. 15, https://www.marxists.org/archive/marx/works/subject/quotes/index.htm.

8. Teresa of Calcutta, "Called to Profess, Not Success," Catholic Life, March 28, 2017, https://catholiclife.diolc.org/2017/03/28/called-to-profess-not-success/.

9. Harry J. Holzer, R. Glenn Hubbard, and Michael R. Strain, "Did Pandemic Unemployment Benefits Reduce Employment? Evidence from Early State-Level Expirations in June 2021," NBER Working Paper Series, National Bureau of Economic Research, December 2021, https://www.nber.org/system/files/working_papers/w29575/w29575.pdf; Peter Ganong *et al.,* "Micro and Macro Disincentive Effects of Expanded Unemployment Benefits," July 29, 2021, https://www.jpmorganchase.com/content/dam/jpmc/jpmorgan-chase-and-co/institute/pdf/when-unemployment-insurance-benefits-are-rolled-back-paper.pdf.

10. John Paul II, *Centesimus annus*, The Vatican, May 1, 1991, https://www.vatican.va/content/john-paul-ii/en/encyclicals/documents/hf_jp-ii_enc_01051991_centesimus-annus.html, section 48.

11. John P. Meier, *A Marginal Jew* vol. 5, *Probing the Authenticity of the Parables* (New Haven, Connecticut: Yale University Press, 2016), 291. For a good analysis of the failure of the third servant, see Klyne Snodgrass, *Stories with Intent: A Comprehensive Guide to the Parables of Jesus* (Grand Rapids, Michigan: William B. Eerdmans, 2008), 532.

Chapter 8: *The King Going to War*

1. *Catechism of the Catholic Church* 2309, Catholic Culture, https://www.catholicculture.org/culture/library/catechism/index.cfm?recnum=1673.

2. For a classic discussion of why socialistic economic arrangements make economic calculation impossible, see Ludwig von Mises, *Socialism: An Economic and Sociological Analysis* (London: Jonathan Cape, 1974), 131, where he succinctly sums up his argument: "Where there is no market, there is no price

system, and where there is no price system there can be no economic calculation."

3. See my discussion of this in the Afterword.

Chapter 9: *The House Built on a Rock*

1. Joachim Jeremias, *Rediscovering the Parables* (New York: Charles Scribner's Sons, 1968), 153.

Chapter 10: *Lessons in Stewardship*

1. Arland J. Hultgren, *The Parables of Jesus: A Commentary* (Grand Rapids, Michigan: William B. Eerdmans Publishing Company, 2000), 159.
2. Leopold Fonck, *The Parables of Christ: An Exegetical and Practical Explanation*, ed. George O'Neill (Fort Collins, Colorado: Roman Catholic Books, 1997), 403.
3. For an elaboration on the way in which command and control economies frustrate economic coordination, see F. A. Hayek, *The Fatal Conceit: The Errors of Socialism*, ed. W.W . Bartley (Chicago: University of Chicago Press, 1988).
4. Pablo Gadenz, *Catholic Commentary on Sacred Scripture: The Gospel of Luke* (Grand Rapids, Michigan: Baker Academic, 2018), 282.
5. Thomas Aquinas, *Summa Theologica*, II–II q. 47 a. 2 ad. 1.

Chapter 11: *The Good Samaritan*

1. Flavius Josephus, *The Antiquities of the Jews*, trans. William Whiston (Blacksburg, Virginia: Unabridged Books, 2011), Chapters 12–20.
2. Cf. Klyne Snodgrass, *Stories with Intent: A Comprehensive Guide to the Parables of Jesus* (Grand Rapids, Michigan: William B. Eerdmans, 2008), 347; Arland J. Hultgren, *The Parables of Jesus: A Commentary* (Grand Rapids, Michigan: William B. Eerdmans Publishing Company, 2000), 99.
3. Benedict XVI, *Jesus of Nazareth: From the Baptism in Jordan to the Transfiguration*, trans. Adrian J. Walker (New York: Doubleday, 2007), 196.
4. Francis, *Fratelli tutti*, The Vatican, October 3, 2020, https://www.vatican.va/content/francesco/en/encyclicals/documents/papa-francesco_20201003_enciclica-fratelli-tutti.html.
5. Benedict XVI, *Deus caritas est*, The Vatican, 2005, http://www.vatican.va/content/benedict-xvi/en/encyclicals/documents/hf_ben-xvi_enc_20051225_deus-caritas-est.html, section 28.
6. John Paul II, *Centesimus annus*, The Vatican, May 1, 1991, http://www.vatican.va/content/john-paul-ii/en/encyclicals/documents/hf_jp-ii_enc_01051991_ce

ntesimus-annus.html, section 48. "In recent years the range of such intervention has vastly expanded, to the point of creating a new type of State, the so-called 'Welfare State.' This has happened in some countries in order to respond better to many needs and demands, by remedying forms of poverty and deprivation unworthy of the human person. However, excesses and abuses, especially in recent years, have provoked very harsh criticisms of the Welfare State, dubbed the 'Social Assistance State.' Malfunctions and defects in the Social Assistance State are the result of an inadequate understanding of the tasks proper to the State. Here again *the principle of subsidiarity* must be respected: a community of a higher order should not interfere in the internal life of a community of a lower order, depriving the latter of its functions, but rather should support it in case of need and help to coordinate its activity with the activities of the rest of society, always with a view to the common good. By intervening directly and depriving society of its responsibility, the Social Assistance State leads to a loss of human energies and an inordinate increase of public agencies, which are dominated more by bureaucratic ways of thinking than by concern for serving their clients, and which are accompanied by an enormous increase in spending. In fact, it would appear that needs are best understood and satisfied by people who are closest to them and who act as neighbours to those in need. It should be added that certain kinds of demands often call for a response which is not simply material but which is capable of perceiving the deeper human need. One thinks of the condition of refugees, immigrants, the elderly, the sick, and all those in circumstances which call for assistance, such as drug abusers: all these people can be helped effectively only by those who offer them genuine fraternal support, in addition to the necessary care."

7. Benedict XVI, *Jesus of Nazareth*, 199.

Chapter 12: *The Rich Man and Lazarus*

1. Bernard Brandon Scott, *Hear Then the Parable: A Commentary on the Parables of Jesus* (Minneapolis, Minnesota: Fortress Press, 1990), 151.

2. Ernesto Cardenal, *The Gospel in Solentiname* vol. 3 (Maryknoll, New York: Orbis, 1972), 252.

3. For examples of billionaires losing huge amounts of money, see Deniz Çam, "The Biggest Billionaire Winners and Losers of 2019," *Forbes*, December 20, 2019, https://www.forbes.com/sites/denizcam/2019/12/20/the-biggest-billiona ire-winners-and-losers-of-2019/#4dc47bcc3ec2; Erin McDowell, "These 10 Billionaires Have All Gone Broke or Declared Bankruptcy—Read the Wild Stories of How They Lost Their Fortunes," *Business Insider*, March 26, 2020,

https://www.businessinsider.com/rich-billionaires-who-declared-bankruptcy
-2019-7; Adrián Francisco Varela and Qayyah Moynihan, "17 Billionaires Who
Lost the Most in the Past Year," *Business Insider*, January 23, 2019, https://
www.businessinsider.com/the-17-billionaires-who-made-the-biggest-losses-in
-the-past-year-2018-2019-1.

Chapter 13: *The Prodigal Son*

1. John Nolland, "The Role of Money and Possessions in the Parable of the
    Prodigal Son (Luke 18:11–32)," in Craig G. Bartholomew, Joel B. Green, and
    Anthony C. Thiselton, *Reading Luke: Interpretation, Reflection, Formation*,
    Scripture and Hermenetuics 7 (Grand Rapids, Michigan: Zondervan, 2005),
    178–209.
2. Klyne Snodgrass, *Stories with Intent: A Comprehensive Guide to the Parables of
    Jesus* (Grand Rapids, Michigan: William B. Eerdmans Publishing Company,
    2008), 131.
3. In essence, this is the point that Nolland makes when he observes that the
    parable "explores the tension between the concerns of justice, which are part of
    the classic wisdom perspective and the importance and desirability of family
    reconciliation." Nolland, "The Role of Money and Possessions," 204.
4. Snodgrass, *Stories with Intent*, 139.
5. Joachim Jeremias, *The Parables of Jesus Second Revised Edition* (Hoboken, New
    Jersey: Prentice Hall, 1972), 130.
6. Snodgrass, *Stories with Intent*, 124.

Afterword: *Some Broader Thoughts on Economics and the New Testament*

1. See Alejandro Chafuen, *Faith and Liberty: The Economic Thought of the Late
    Scholastics*, 2nd ed. (Lanham, Maryland: Lexington Books, 2003); Raymond de
    Roover, *Business, Banking, and Economic Thought in Late Medieval and Early
    Modern Europe* (Chicago: University of Chicago Press, 1975); Joseph
    Schumpeter, *History of Economic Analysis* (Oxford: Oxford University Press,
    1996).
2. *Revised Standard Version* (New York: The Division of Christian Education of
    the National Council of the Churches of Christ in the United States of America,
    1971).
3. Augustine of Hippo, *The Confessions*, trans. F. J. Sheed (Indianapolis, Indiana:
    Hackett Publishing Co., 2006).

4. Philippians 4:11–13, *Revised Standard Version Catholic Edition* (San Francisco, California: Ignatius Press, 1994).

5. Philippians 4:11–13, *The Amplified Bible* (Grand Rapids, Michigan: Zondervan, 2017).

6. Fifty-two percent of the world's population lived in absolute poverty in 1981; by 2005, only 25 percent did, according to World Bank figures. See Daniel Griswold, *Mad about Trade: Why Main Street America Should Embrace Globalization* (Washington, D.C.: Cato Institute, 2009), 127.

7. Keith O. Fuglie, James M. MacDonald, and Eldon Ball, *Productivity Growth in U.S. Agriculture, Economic Brief* no. 9 (September 2007), https://www.ers.usda.gov/webdocs/publications/42924/11854_eb9_1_.pdf.

8. Second Vatican Council, *Gaudium et spes*, no. 26, The Vatican, https://www.vatican.va/archive/hist_councils/ii_vatican_council/documents/vat-ii_const_19651207_gaudium-et-spes_en.html.

9. It is at least worth noting that while Jesus commands the young man to *sell* and "give to the poor" in each of the synoptic accounts, in none of them is it clear that he is being told to give *all* the proceeds of this sale to the poor, only to "give to the poor".

10. David Bentley Hart, "Mammon Ascendent," *First Things* (June 2016).

11. Joseph Fitzmyer, *The Gospel According to Luke*, vol. 2 (New York: Doubleday, 1981–1985), 1109.

12. José Porfirio Miranda, *Communism in the Bible* (Maryknoll, New York: Orbis, 1992).

13. *Gregory the Great: Homilies on the Gospel of St. Luke*, 40:2 as cited in Francis Fernandez, *In Conversation with God: Meditations for Each Day of the Year*, vol. 2 (Strongsville, Ohio: Scepter Publishing, 1989).

14. Craig Blomberg "Jesus, Sinners, and Table Fellowship," *Bulletin for Biblical Research* 19, no. 1 (2009): 35–62.

15. See Matthew 9:11, Mark 2:16, and Luke 5:30.

16. Joseph Ratzinger, *Jesus of Nazareth: Holy Week* (San Francisco: Ignatius Press, 2011), 13–16.

17. Ched Myers, *Binding the Strong Man: A Political Reading of Mark's Story of Jesus* (Maryknoll, New York: Orbis Books, 2017).

18. Ibid., 300.

19. Ibid., 301.

20. Klyne R. Snodgrass, "The Temple Incident" *in Key Events in the Life of the Historical Jesus: A Collaborative Exploration of Context and Coherence*, ed.

Darrell L. Bock and Robert L. Webb (Tübingen, Germany: Mohr Siebeck, 2009), 455–60.

21. Raymond Brown et al., *The New Jerome Biblical Commentary* (Englewood, New Jersey: Prentice Hall, 1990), 664; Joachim Jeremias, *Jerusalem in the Time of Jesus* (Philadelphia, Pennsylvania: Fortress Press, 1969), 33.

22. Curtis Mitch and Edward Sri, *Catholic Commentary on Sacred Scripture: The Gospel of Matthew* (Grand Rapids, Michigan: Baker Publishing, 2010), 269–70.

23. Cf. Zechariah 14:21.

24. Frederick Engels, "On the History of Early Christianity," Marxists Internet Archive, https://www.marxists.org/archive/marx/works/1894/early-christianity/index.htm.

25. David Bentley Hart, "Are Christians Supposed to Be Communists?," *New York Times*, November 4, 2017, https://www.nytimes.com/2017/11/04/opinion/sunday/christianity-communism.html.

26. Luke Timothy Johnson, *The Literary Function of Possessions in Luke-Acts* (Dissertation series, Society of Biblical Literature), (Missoula, Montana: Scholars Press, 1977): 39.

27. Ibid., 10, note 3.

28. Ibid., 136.

29. Ibid., 139.

30. I am grateful to my Acton Institute colleague Dylan Pahman for his observations on this matter.